AMERICA'S OLDEST PROFESSIONS

WARRING AND SPYING

By Gary Brumback

I0411229

Revised Edition
Forward by David Swanson

America's Oldest Professions: Warring and Spying
Revised Edition
Copyright © 2015 by Gary Brumback
LCCN 2015903150

PRAISE FOR THE BOOK FROM WWII AND LATER VETERANS

Dr. Brumback gives us a penetrating exposé of an America in the late stages of an addiction. The toll of death, destruction and human misery from its habitual warring and spying is mounting. However, before any cure can be undertaken, there must be a thorough diagnosis. His cutting incisiveness leaves little doubt about the necessity for what must be done if America is to avoid one or more dismal to catastrophic scenarios he foresees in the near to distant future. He moves us from the historic onset of the disease, through its insidious life-threatening rise, culminating with his proposed seven-step reform to end the addiction.

--- Hal O'Leary, WWII veteran who now, in his prolific writing, denounces all wars.

"Brumback has packed much into this short work for both veteran peace activists and those newly realizing that America is not a beacon of hope for freedom but an imperial power bent on global domination. He concisely summarizes all the fallacies inherent in the concept of "national defense" in a unipolar world where the only threat to the United States is the hubris of its so-called "leaders." A unique contribution is his challenge to the notion that the spying industry has any function but to promote the imperialist agenda of those who dictate foreign policy of the US government, to the detriment of both the citizens of targeted nations and Americans themselves. Brumback demolishes the arguments for "just" and "necessary" wars, dissects the roots of imperialism in spying and war, and provides a recipe for ending America's spying and wars and that the American public would do well to follow."

3

--- Rick Staggenborg, MD, Army veteran, former VA psychiatrist resigned to run for the US Senate in 2010 on a pledge to introduce a Constitutional amendment to reform campaign finance. He now works full time for the educational nonprofit Take Back America for the People and with the world network of justice activists, Soldiers For Peace International.

To today's American citizen, it seems quite normal to have our soldiers stationed across the world and engaged in frequent, if not on-going military conflict. We are proud of having the world's best military, and are willing to pay for it. We are told that we need a massive intelligence network to keep us safe and we believe that too, but has it always been this way? In America's Oldest Professions, author Gary Brumback traces the long history of this country's obsession with warring and spying, calling them two "habits" that need breaking. Are warring and spying inherent parts of what makes this country what it is? Is this what we want? Do we have the power to change it? Important questions for sure, and Brumback helps us begin to answer them.

---Leah Bolger retired from the U.S. Navy at the rank of Commander after twenty years of active duty service. She was elected as the first female President of Veterans For Peace in 2012, and in 2013 was selected to present the Ava Helen and Linus Pauling Memorial Peace Lecture at Oregon State University. She currently serves as the Chair of the Coordinating Committee of "World Beyond War," an international coalition to abolish war.

Dr. Brumback's book demonstrates just how inured this nation has become to war for war's sake. I would hope that his observations and his solutions would become a must read for the general public, but after trying endlessly to reach people through my own writing, I fear that only those that already know how far down the "rabbit hole" we have traveled will ever gaze upon this book. Dr Brumback is a moralist in the true sense of the word. It is through voices like his that may bring us back from the abyss. I encourage any of you that obtain this book to pass it around.

---Timothy Gatto, former Chairman of the Liberal Party of America, a retired Army Sergeant, author of Kimchee Days (or Stoned Cold Warriors) and From Complicity to Contempt, talk radio host, and Assistant Editor of The Oliver Arts and Open Press.

I'm very much impressed with both Gary Brumback's book content as well as his writing style. Each chapter flows effortlessly and seamlessly, making complete sense of the whole truth about America's two most debilitating and destructive habits - war and spying. He takes on these two extremely heavy subjects like no other approach out there, with both insightful, matter-of-fact truth and light, heady humor. It's the kind of truth primer most needed as a US history lesson for educating both our young and old alike. Finally, it immediately inspires us readers to want to take mindful action as peace activists in order to rectify the collision course our megalomaniacal leaders that include my West Point peers currently have us racing towards with breakneck speed. I strongly recommend this gem of a truth nugget to every human being on earth who embraces life over death.

---Joachim Hagopian is a West Point graduate and former US Army officer. He has written a manuscript based on his unique military experience entitled "West Point Exposed: The Militarization of the World." As the first cadet to successfully challenge the totalitarian system at our most honored institution, Joachim's legal case forced West Point to no longer operate above the law, imposing due process on its previously impenetrable gray stone walls. After the military, Joachim earned a Master's degree in Clinical Psychology and worked as a licensed therapist in the mental health field for more than a quarter century. As an investigative journalist, Joachim is now writing articles exposing the truth about the American Empire, regularly contributing to the Global Research E-Newsletter.

PRAISE FOR THE BOOK FROM OTHERS

America's Oldest Profession is a terrific book!!! It is a delightful, playful (as in the book's main title) yet sobering, and insightful description of America's addiction to war and spying. Conversational but controversial, Brumback depicts a nation born with a musket and a spy glass wrecking havoc around the world. His 7-step program to break the US addiction is simple, elegant and inspirational—a clear blueprint for a more creative and effective peace movement. Read it and act now before it could be too late.
---Medea Benjamin, cofounder, CODEPINK for Peace, international peace activist, author of Drone Warfare: Killing by Remote Control, and many other books, recipient of many peace awards, a nominee for the Nobel Peace Prize in 2010, and the Green Party candidate for U.S. Senate from California in 2000.

Brumback has written a folksy, easy and fun to read exposé on the dark underbelly of America's history and current events: endless wars and spying. His meticulously researched and referenced resources reflect a serious scholarship about a deadly serious subject that needs the attention of every American concerned about America's future,

---Jeff J. Brown, author of "44 Days Backpacking in China" and his forthcoming "Reflections in Sinoland – Reporting from the Belly of the New Century Beast"

Gary Brumback not only hit a home run with his book, America's Oldest Professions, he hit a grand slam home run. He takes two themes, persistent spying and warfare, and meticulously demonstrates how the nation's history has been interwoven and developed by using these two main themes. The author was more than meticulous in his research, and thoroughly documents his supportive evidence to construct his historical contentions. Like one of his heroes Howard Zinn, this book sheds tremendous light on the other facets of history that do appear in traditional textbooks. This is a look at the dark side but amazingly well documented. Like Zinn's book, this should be required reading in any study of American history. In addition, the author offers a thought provoking plan to rectify the problems he so thoroughly enumerated in his book. While extensively documented, the author's style flows easily, resulting in a very informative readable book.

---Joe Clifford who lives in Rhode Island taught American history at the high school level and writes regulars columns for 3 online newspapers. His articles deal almost primarily with American Foreign policy, but ventures into other areas of concern relevant to the current American scene.

In 'America's Oldest Professions,' Brumback imagines something that no one alive today has ever experienced: a United States that abstains from war and spying. Brumback leverages his characteristic passion and incisive analysis to document how America's status quo came to be, and leads us to consider what an 'Alter-America'

without war and espionage might look like. Whether or not you agree with him, Brumback will make you think!"
--- S. Bartholomew ("Bart") Craig is an associate professor of industrial-organizational psychology at North Carolina State University, where he teaches and researches organizational leadership and other subjects. His work is published in numerous scholarly journals and books, and presented at national conferences. He is on the editorial boards of two journals and is former editor of the Book Review Section for Personnel Psychology. He coauthored the Perceived Leader Integrity Scale for assessing leaders' ethical integrity.

Do you ever notice how popular it is in America to use the word "war?" When I grew up during the tail end of the Vietnam War, that word "war" was a dirty word, but how soon we forget those ideals and allow the government to "patriotize" us into one war after another, and gladly give up our civil liberties as well. As Dr. Gary Brumback points out it his book, America's Oldest Professions: Warring and Spying, these two activities are business activities for my country. Business activities which cost taxpayers trillions of dollars and result in inexcusable losses of lives in the thousands for Americans, and the hundreds of thousands or even millions of others, many of them innocent. The drone program is only one abhorrent example of assassinations taking place as we speak in other parts of the world, at which we are not even at war, and resulting in innocent losses of life that our government shrugs off as "collateral damage."
--- Kenneth Gordon Eade is an American environmental activist, author and lawyer, best known for his legal and political thrillers (e.g., A Patriot's Act).

If you want an insight as to how your country, the U.S. of A., actually works, this book was written for you. I follow politics closely, and this book connected dots together for me on every page. Astoundingly well researched (footnoted at the end of the chapters), with clear and concise writing. If you liked Howard Zinn, whom Gary considers his mentor, you will surely like this book. The insights into "what makes this country run," and has since its inception will surely open your eyes, astound and likely horrify you, but also, hopefully, motivate you to do what you can to become active from whatever position you are in in this society.

--- Daniel Geery lived for 15 years on solar power in an earth-sheltered house; he volunteered on environmental and energy projects for decades, including running for Federal Senator from Utah; he taught elementary school for a quarter century. Currently he writes political articles and is working on an airship that has attracted worldwide attention, due to its implications for the future of aviation.

Brumback pulls no punches in this incisive and thorough analysis of our government's long history of waging overseas wars and spying on its own citizens. This book should be required reading in every political science and history class and recommended to the general public since most Americans have no clue of the evildoings perpetuated by their own government. The book includes a comprehensive plan for breaking the regime's warring and spying habits and provides dismal scenarios of the future if the habits aren't broken.

--- Arlen Grossman, writer and blogger, editor of the political blog The Big Picture Report.

Gary Brumback has written a remarkable and insightful book that merits a wide readership. "Warring"and "Spying" have led this republic to the brink of destruction and this book is determined to lead us away from the precipice.

--- Gerald Horne, distinguished Chair of History and African American Studies at the University of Houston, author of 'The Counter-Revolution of 1776: Slave Resistance and the Origins of the USA' and 30 some other books.

Brumback tells us politicians and their donors, the war and spy industries, will never voluntarily stop their addiction to warring and spying. He proposes a plan for ending the addiction and warns us that doing nothing guarantees a frightening future. His book is a must read for all Americans either oblivious to or worried about that future.
---Rob Kall, founder and publisher of OpEdNnews.com, originator and host of the Bottom-up Radio, 1360AM, Huffington Post bloggers, and new social media consultant.

Gary Brumback seems to be one of the very few conscientious human beings working hard to help free the world of America's chronic, costly and deadly warring and spying habits. I found this book to be both challenging and helpful to those of us who are awake and care about what is happening. It is a highly moral work that gives us a non-violent seven-step plan for creating an "Alter America," an America that has found the strength to re-invent itself in order to build a better future and fulfill a better destiny than what we now are experiencing.
---Daniel Penisten, retired warehouse worker, author of the American Earned Guaranteed Income, and advocate of a cultural transformation of America.

Gary Brumback has done all of humanity a service by writing this book. Not only does he point out the insanity of the emperors' naked pursuit of war and conquest, he tells us what to do about it. I especially commend his 7-step "Alter America" program–including the call for a

Citizens' Assembly for Peace and for all of us to get personally involved in peace-making.
--- Fran Quigley, Clinical Professor, Health and Human Rights Clinic, Indiana University Robert H. McKinney School of Law, author of How Human Rights Can Build Haiti: Activists, Lawyers, and the Grassroots Campaign, and other books.

Do you want the truth? Can you handle the truth? Gary Brumback powerfully lays it out as he demolishes age-old revered myths, now deeply entrenched in our psyches. With incisiveness and candor he tracks the genesis and history to the present of two poisons in the arteries of America, war and spying. While always dangerous, these traditional pillars of Americanism have now achieved an addictive grip on our foreign policy, economy, every aspect of our lives, such that we now find ourselves plunging toward the destruction of the moral fabric of our nation, and probably its demise.
---John Rachel has a BA in Philosophy, is widely traveled, and author of eight novels and hundreds of political essays published in print and online.

Gary Brumback has written a book that lays bare the troubling truth that wars, like government lies, are not occasional aberrations in the normal course of American society but "business as usual"; a constant and ongoing stream of conflict which bring the authors of such conflicts immediate riches and power at the expense of everyone else. This book is a wake-up call to all Americans that the time has come to abandon our childhood beliefs in truthful and peace-loving leadership and acknowledge the true nature of our government as greedy, rapacious, and unjustly aggressive towards other nations and other people. World War One, sold to the people as "The War to End All Wars," brought great riches to the bankers and

11

industrialists of the winning nations, such that it was only a few decades before World War Two was created for the same purpose. As we hover at the precipice of yet another global conflict, Brumback's book is a window into the true motives behind the constant state of war carried out by the United States.

----Michael Rivero, creator of whatreallyhappened.com, now in its 20th year, host of a talk radio show on the Genesis Communications Network, worked at NASA and visual effects and computer animation for film and TV until blacklisted for his political activism, and a peace activist who lives in Hawaii with his wife Claire, a composer, contributor to the website and co-owner of their Homebaked Entertainment Radio and TV Commercials business, and a peace activist.

Gary Brumback has written a hard hitting book that hones in on a very important concept: addiction. Indeed America is addicted to warring and spying. The predators who rule are power addicts. Like all addicts they constantly seek the next high, and are constantly lying in the service of their addiction. America's Oldest Professions is a book written with compassion and outrage, in an easy to read, conversational style. It is energizing. It is empowering. Brumback offers some practical suggestions for how to bring an end to perpetual war for perpetual peace, for which he deserves congratulations. There are several fact-packed appendices at the end.

---Arthur D. Robbins is the author of Paradise Lost, Paradise Regained: The True Meaning of Democracy, referred to by Ralph Nader as, "An eye-opening, earth-shaking book . . . a fresh, torrential shower of revealing insights and vibrant lessons . . ." and the recently released e-book based on Part II of Paradise Lost entitled,

Democracy Denied: The Untold Story. To learn more visit acropolis-newyork.com

Gary Brumback's remarkable study America's Oldest Professions weaves together truths we need in order to repair our diseased value system. Indeed, warring and spying are both forms of prostitution, which certainly comes out ahead—making love, not war. Brumback does bring in masculine values as abettors of violence, pointing to how few women throughout known history have been world powers and that those who were, were too infected with the Weltanschauung they were born into—to wit, for a few examples, Maggie Thatcher and Madeleine Albright. In a brief hour he has shaken up my world like an earthquake and shifted my priorities. His words, ideas, and worlds must transcend the printed page. Read it, pass it along, and let the ideas empower you to work harder the harder it gets. Yes, we can, despite 4,000 years away from the peace of matriarchy, save the world from our "badvantageous" selves!
---Marta Steele, blogger, former college professor, editor, peace activist, author of several hundred online articles, and author of Grassroots, Geeks, Pros and Pols: The Election Integrity Movement's Rise and Nonstop Battle to Win Back the People's Vote, 2000-2008.

Dr. Gary Brumback has written a gem. In America's Oldest Professions: Warring and Spying, he presents a meticulous expose of America's wars, from the birth of the nation through to the present, shattering the propagandist "America is a democracy" myth, calling it instead a corpocracy, wherein corporations, not people, rule. And if you thought that spying was a recent US phenomenon, Dr. Brumback effectively disavows that. The readability aspect of this book is huge – as if the author dropped in for tea and a chat. It flows along –

uncluttered, cohesive, informative, analytical, researched (it is chock full of footnotes listed after every chapter!) That so much information is contained within a very short book speaks highly to Dr. Brumback's writing ability and scholarship. His seven step strategy to break this war/spy cycle is enlightening, progressive and, most importantly, achievable.

--- Angie Tibbs, writer, activist and Senior Editor at Dissident Voice.

I am in awe. What an achievement! I can only imagine the enormous amount of time and effort Dr. Brumback put into building this cogent and compelling argument for peace. In his book, organized religion is considered one of several "habit helpers," having provided "the 'spiritual motivation' and the spiritual rationalizations for wars and violence ever since deities were invented..." Dr. Brumback asks: "No matter what their faith, how many religious leaders in America can we expect to tell their flocks to protest America's warring and spying habits?" That question reflects a driving hypothesis of my own work: that mainstream religion is the only force on the planet capable of achieving peace. Working together, religious folks have the power to literally save the world; working at odds, they have the power to destroy it. Dr. Brumback envisions an "Alter America" at peace with the world, and offers a thoughtful seven-step plan for achieving that vision. If religious folk in America can work together for peace, Gary Brumback has a plan.

---John Tierney, PhD, retired psychologist, Executive Director at the Peaceful Educator Foundation, author of On Being Human and The Book, composer, professional trombonist and flautist, and educator.

Gary Brumback is an excellent writer. There is a wealth of information in this book that could easily be a multivolume series. The author traces and explains the nearly 240 year old history of America's warring and spying; offers a way to break these chronic, costly and deadly habits; and describes dismal to catastrophic scenarios if these habits are not broken. I appreciated that throughout the book a human face to events and decisions has been provided.

--- Rowan Wolf, Ph.D.,sociologist, writer, and Editor in Chief of Cyrano's Journal.

CONTENTS

FORWARD

One of the ways in which we commonly handicap our own struggles to reform the bad practices of the U.S. government is by imagining those practices to be degenerative developments taking us away from a purer and nobler past. As Gary Brumback shows in this book, the United States grew out of the idea that (in Thomas Paine's phrase) it was "common sense" to launch a war to settle political differences, a war that in turn set the new nation free to launch a series of wars against the indigenous people of the continent, followed quickly by a ceaseless string of wars waged in near and far-flung corners of the globe.

This deeply moral, highly readable, and urgently necessary book, which provides a wealth of new information even to a reader like myself who writes on similar topics, takes us from the birth of the United States to the Barack Obama presidency. Brumback documents George Washington's role as first warrior in chief and first chief spy, and traces that legacy through some 13,000 to 14,000 U.S. military wars/interventions since, operations that have killed some 20 million to 30 million foreign civilians just in the years after World War II, and that have killed more than two and a half million U.S. soldiers over nearly two and a half centuries.

Brumback's argument is not for "just wars" or more competent spying but for a shift away from these practices. War destroys the natural environment, wastes trillions of dollars, and has no upside. All militarism and spying cost the U.S. government well over $1 trillion a year and rising. In exchange for this investment, which at least matches if it does not exceed the rest of the world combined, the United States leads wealthy nations in inequality, unemployment, food insecurity, life expectancy, prison population, homelessness, and other measures of what all the militarism is supposedly protecting: a way of life.

We've been trained to think of war preparations -- and the wars that result from being so incredibly prepared for wars -- as necessary if regrettable. What if, however, in the long view that this book allows us, war turns out to be counterproductive on its own terms? What if war endangers those who wage it rather than protecting them? Imagine, for a moment, how many countries Canada would have to invade and occupy before it could successfully generate anti-Canadian terrorist networks to rival the hatred and resentment currently organized against the United States.

Brumback goes further, documenting that spying is as useless and counterproductive on its own terms as war is. Most secrets sought and maintained by the U.S. government have literally no strategic value even in terms of the militarist thinking that drives the spying. The CIA straddles the space between keystone cop performances of handing nuclear plans to Iran or grounding flights because a con artist claims to see secret terrorist messages in television broadcasts, and the deadly anti-democratic destruction of overthrowing governments and murdering innocent people with drone strikes. In a "free market" competition, the CIA or the Pentagon would lose out to an agency that did literally nothing, much less to a department that worked toward peace, justice, and stability through nonviolent means.

So, what drives what has come to look like war for the sake of war and spying for the sake of spying? Brumback proposes the useful term "badvantages" to categorize features of U.S. society that are not necessarily "roots" or "causes" of war but which facilitate war when found in combination. This section of the book provides an excellent outline of the military industrial spying congressional complex and analysis of how it functions. Greed, obedience, and banal immorality play central roles.

As I write these words, the U.S. Congress is missing in action, having fled Washington in order to allow a new war to begin without holding a vote on whether or not to authorize it. Weapons stocks are at record heights on Wall Street, and a financial advisor on National Public Radio was just heard recommending investing in weaponry.

Banksters come in for a healthy dose of criticism as a badvantage, as do the think tanks that just can't stop thinking about tanks. Also exposed to the light in these pages are front groups for war interests, war supporters in religion and especially in education, patriotic festivals, news media, Hollywood, war toys, the domestic U.S. gun industry, academia, and -- last but not least -- people who do nothing, or "accessories after the fact." That's a lot of badvantages to be overcome.

Often, of course, it is after the fact -- after the launching of a new war -- that people come around to opposing it. For 70 years somewhere upwards of 90 percent of Americans who argue that war can be just or necessary have gone primarily to World War II as evidence for their claim. Never mind that World War II is unimaginable without

World War I which nobody thinks was necessary. Never mind the support that Wall Street and the U.S. State Department gave to the Nazis for years leading up to the crisis. For 70 years people have imagined that, like World War II, some new war might be a good one. This hope has lasted for weeks or months and then faded. For most of the duration of the 2003-2011 U.S.-led war on Iraq, a U.S. majority said it should never have been started. In this sense, it is "accessories before the fact" who are hurting us the most.

Brumback envisions another way of addressing ourselves to the world, in which we would lose the idea that War #14,001 might finally be the good one that fulfills the promises of World War I and trails peace and prosperity behind its bombs and poisons. He also recommends a comprehensive series of steps to move us in that direction. This book is worth whatever you paid for it for its concluding sections alone. The creation of a Citizens Assembly for Peace is, I think, exactly the way to go, although I'm not so sure it should be national. An assembly composed of citizens of the world has potential, I believe. In either case, building such a structure is project number one. We do not need a better Obama, a change of face in a position that corrupts absolutely. We need a better Occupy, a bigger broader bolder movement that finally resorts to the most powerful tool in our arsenal: nonviolence."

David Swanson is an author, activist, journalist, and radio host. He is director of WorldBeyondWar.org and campaign coordinator forRootsAction.org. Swanson's books include War Is A Lie. He blogs at DavidSwanson.org and WarIsACrime.org. He hosts Talk Nation Radio.

PREFACE

The oldest professions? No, but "America's Second Oldest Professions" would have been a salacious title, and salacious this book is not. So I took a literary license. No license is needed however to say that America was born with a musket and spy glass in her hands and that she has never let go of them, never broken those two addictive, chronic, and costly habits. The toll of death, destruction, and human misery from her warring and spying over nearly 240 years is mounting as you read this.

Contrary to what has been written and said in nearly 240 years of America's lore, doctrine, propaganda, and sanitized education, America was not born to be the land of the free, the land of plenty, and the land of opportunity nor is she the leader of the free world. Those descriptions are mostly slogans and political propaganda, not widespread realities except for the privileged and power elite. That exception was the deliberate aim of her "founding fathers," plutocrats who were not about to design and build a truly representative democracy, one that embraced the unwashed masses. Who knew that better than the Native Americans, the slaves, the indentured servants, the women? America was led astray by her leaders from the get go and the misleading has never stopped.

The colonists fought their way free of King George's corpocracy only to let their leaders perpetuate it at home, a government not of, by and for the people but a government in collusion with and controlled by powerful corporate interests. I have called that collusion a "corpocracy," " and I wrote a book about it [1]. America's hypocrisy began when she began, an oligarchy turning into a copocracy all the while pretending to be a democracy.

This corporacy, which I sometimes also call America's regime, is responsible for America's lowest standing among so-called "advanced" countries on everything that matters: unemployment rate; prevalence of poverty; income inequality; quality of health and health care; quality of and demographics of education; homelessness; you name it. [2] The most ominous for the future of America are her warring and spying addictions that are part and parcel of the corpocracy. Unless America can break those two habits she could someday be broken herself.

About this Book

This book is about those two addictive habits; their long history, what explains them, what their consequences are, how they can be broken, and what awaits America and the world if they are not broken.

Chapter1 traces the unbroken history of the two habits. Chapter 2 documents their costs and consequences. It is an appalling account of the damage and death America's warriors-in-chiefs and spy chiefs have unceasingly caused America and elsewhere on the globe. Chapter 3 explains the warring and spying habits. You will read there about the "black boxes" and "badvantages" that explain the dark side of human behavior in general and the warring and spying habits of the current U.S. president and his predecessor in particular. Chapter 4 examines the war and spy bureaucracy of the U.S. government. There we will look into the public officialdom of the two habits, The Land of the Official Habbits, if you will, with apologies to J.R.R Tolkien. Chapter 5 examines the war and spy industries that feed off government's addiction as well as their own. You will read there how contractors go about milking Uncle Sam, and how Uncle Sam, the reliable cash cow, knows and doesn't care. Chapter 6 takes a look at the "Habit Helpers." You might be surprised about who some of them are. I was once one of them. Chapter 7 proposes a seven-step program for ending America's warring and spying. The last chapter presents some dismal scenarios of the future if the habits aren't ended. In the Afterword are developments and discussions arising after the chapters were written. Be sure not to miss Appendix A, especially if you believe there can be a just or necessary war. In Appendix B we "hear" imminent voices against war down through the ages. Appendix C shows the bloated organizational chart for the war and spy agencies, and Appendix D names the largest war and spy contractors.

I have tried to write the book in a conversational style, my talking directly to you the reader. This style is a big departure from my earlier years of writing in academic circles. Speaking of habits, that one was hard to break (but I haven't broken the habit of loading up on footnotes as you will see). I have also tried to be as humorous as possible when appropriate, starting with the book's title, without making light of a very serious subject. Life is too short not to grin and laugh once in a while, wouldn't you agree? But if you think the book is more controversial than conversational and humorous I would agree with you.

What is not humorous or controversial is that millions upon millions of the terminal victims of America's warring and spying will never breathe again, let alone laugh. Regardless of whether they were Americans or the regime's enemies or bystander victims, they ought to be on every American's conscience, but they aren't. We rightfully mourn our loved ones lost in battle but wrongfully not those of the enemies of America's regimes.

Is this Book Unpatriotic?

Who is patriotic; the corporate CEO and board of directors who milk the government for all the handouts and immunities they can get and then turn around and relocate their company in some foreign country to get even better tax breaks, or critics who say American corporations should stay American and stop their greedy and unscrupulous practices?

Who is patriotic; politicians who buy their votes with corporate financing and yield to corporate lobbyists or critics who say America's politicians should be honest representatives of democracy, not of corpocracy?

Who is patriotic; public officials and the war and spy industries that bomb, bully and snoop, or critics who say those practices are murderous, tyrannical, soil America's image to the world, and invite dangerous blowbacks that harm the American public?

Who is patriotic; a retired general and former director of the CIA and NSA you will read about later who said that "We are gathering data to make America more profitable for more commercial enterprises," or critics who say his agencies' intrusive and invasive spying is illegal and robbing Americans of their right to privacy?

Who is patriotic; people who say "track and kill the enemy with drone strikes," or people who say "America, please stop creating enemies to feed the war and spy business and the corpocracy's desire to control the world's resources?"

Consider which of these two national sentiments helps sustain a nation's warring and spying; "my country right or wrong" or "my country please do right and no wrong"? The first is jingoistic patriotism, or dangerous loyalty. The second is principled patriotism, or cautionary loyalty. Which sentiment prevailed during the Third Reich? Which prevails in America today?

To paraphrase Guy de Maupassant (1850-1893) the great French short story teller of the 19th century, [unprincipled] "patriotism---is the egg from which wars are hatched."

Why I Wrote this Book

I wrote this book because history clearly tells us that U.S. regimes of self-serving politicians and their war and spy collaborators will never voluntarily stop their warring and spying. They won't because they can't. They are addicts.

I wrote this book because America is my homeland, I am a principled patriot, and I want America to be the best homeland she can be for all of her people, not just for the powerful and privileged few. She has the potential to become the Alter America described in Chapter 7, an America where there would be no corpocracy; where she would be peaceful and law abiding; where she would be an egalitarian, not a male dominated society; where her economy depended on Main Street, not on Wall Street; where there would be no more corporate welfare; and where she would be a socially and economically just society. Sound utopian and impossible? It does only if we let it be so.

I wrote this book for other principled patriots. I want this book to galvanize them into making Alter America possible. We can shape America's future but only if we unite, plan, and head toward Alter America. As Ralph Nader once said, "We must strive to become good ancestors."

Comparable Books?

Many books have been written about and against war. Some of them are cited in my footnotes. How does America's Oldest Professions compare to them. Does it offer something different?

Books on any non-fictional subject can seek to answer one or more of these questions: What happened? When did it happen? What preceded or followed it? How did it happen? Why did it happen? What needs to be done about it? America's Oldest Professions gives answers to all of these questions. No other book I have seen does or does it as well in my, albeit biased, opinion.

Consider, for example, two books that give truncated historical accounts of America's war making. One is the New York Times Bestseller and subsequent award winning documentary, Dirty Wars: The World is a Battlefield, by journalist Jeremy Scahill. [3] It is an excellent book, hands down. But its perspective is markedly limited compared to America's Oldest Professions. It is mostly reportorial. Its purpose is not to answer the question why or what can be done about it. The time frame of its subject begins around 1971 and goes to 2011. Much war and bloodshed caused by America came before that period and after it (of course, the book was published in 2013, which probably explains the 2011 cutoff). The other book, by Professor Michel

Chossudovsky, examines America's "long war against humanity," but it is not nearly as long a historical account as America's Oldest Professions. [4] Professor Chossudovsky begins his account after WWII.

Then there are books that focus on specific aspects of America's war making such as drone warfare. I will mention two of them. One is by the internationally famous peace activist Medea Benjamin. [5] There is probably no other non-military citizen who is more knowledgeable on the subject than she is. If drone warfare is ever stopped or banned in America we can thank her. The other book is edited by Marjorie Cohen, an attorney who teaches both international human rights law and criminal law and is a former head of the National Lawyers Guild. [6] Her book, with contributions by a host of experts examines various legal and other issues concerning targeted killing and its impact on America's international relations.

Two other highly acclaimed books I want to mention are not antiwar books per se. Instead, they trace the entire history from pre-civilization forward of conflict and war's supporting cultures and call for a total cultural transformation to unlock us from war. The two are The Chalice and the Blade, and The Real Wealth of Nations, both by Riane Eisler, scholar, writer, and social activist. [7] Her writings have had a profound influence on my thinking. You will see evidence of that influence in Chapter 7 when I describe my vision of Alter America.

I doubt very much that America's Oldest Professions will ever be an award-winning book. I just hope that people who should read my book do read it and become motivated to help implement the plan proposed in Chapter 7.

Dedication

This book is dedicated first to war victims on either side of any conflict. I have a saying, "mourn wars' victims; scorn the war lords.

It is also dedicated to the late Howard Zinn, author of the controversial book on the history of America. [8] History is usually written by the powerful victors, not the powerless losers. Mr. Zinn wrote his book from the losers' perspective. That is why his book is controversial. The powerful hate his book.

Knowledge is power. The ancient Greeks knew that. Everyone knows that who is knowledgeable. People in power who abuse that power absolutely fear the knowledge of truth. That is why there have been so many book and library burnings in history. That is why Mitch Daniels, former governor of my home state, Indiana, good grief, was in a dictatorial dither over Mr. Zinn's book. When Mr. Zinn died at the age of 87, then Governor Daniels wrote to the state's top education officials that "this terrible anti-American academic has finally passed away. A People's History of the United States is a truly execrable, anti-factual piece of disinformation that misstates American history on every page. Can someone assure me that it is not in use anywhere in Indiana? If it is, how do we get rid of it before more young people are force-fed a totally false version of our history." [9] Mr. Daniels stands in a long line of public officials and others responsible for whitewashing the telling and teaching of America's soiled history. [10]

I have read Mr. Zinn's book several times. I have learned more from it than all that I learned from my long formal education eons ago. His book taught me that America has been led astray from her very beginning. And it is still being led astray by the wrong kind of corporate and public leaders showing no sign of charting a different and urgently needed course.

The Mitch Daniels of America will also dislike this book if they bother to read it. For them it would contradict what they have been told by their grandparents, their parents, their teachers, their religious leaders, their government, and the mainstream media. Given "truths" become the convenient "truths" and invariably are at odds with the "inconvenient" truths.

It is regrettable that there are people who accept America for what she is rather than wanting her to become what she should become for the common good because they deliberately want to keep the status quo; they see what they believe; they are compromised like I once was; they feel powerless; they are scared to do anything about it; and/or they care only about themselves.

One gentleman, for example, who looked over an advance copy, told me that he "disagreed with the basic outlook, the negativism about the United States." He is right in the narrowest sense that there is nothing positive about warring and spying, but the book's intent, and the most important part of its content is purely positive. Eliminating the negative requires accentuating both it and the positive alternative.

Appreciation

When I need objective news and analyses about the corpocracy I don't go to the mainstream media controlled by the corpocracy (see Chapter 6). Instead, I rely on investigative journalists and independent outlets, most often AlterNet, The Big Picture Report, William Blum's Anti Empire Report, Corporate Watch, Counterpunch, Crooks and Liars, Cross Currents, Cyrano's Journal, Dissident Voice, Envision This, Global Research E Newsletter, Greanville Post, Huffington Post, The Nation, OpEdNews, PopularResistance.Org Daily Digest, Salon, Tom Dispatch, Truthdig, Truthout, and Waging Nonviolence. Did these journalists and the editorial teams of these outlets and their many indispensable articles not exist neither would this book. I am indebted to them all.

Acknowledgements

I am particularly indebted to the writings and insights of the people cited in the endnotes.

Endnotes

1. Brumback, GB. The Devil's Marriage: Break Up the Corpocracy or Leave Democracy in the Lurch. Author House, 2011.
2. Some sources on America's "sadtistics:" Blow, CM. Empire at the End of Decadence. New York Times, February 18, 2011; Buchheit, P. Five Facts That Put America to Shame. Common Dreams, May 14, 2012; Froomkin, D. Occupy Right Again: U.S. Near Bottom In New Social Justice Index. HuffPostBusiness, October 27, 2011; Sullivan, T. An America In Retreat? Crooks & Liars, July 15, 2013; and Zuesse, E. How the U.S.

Performs in Recent International Rankings; Hint: 3rd, as in Third World. OpEdNews, April 15, 2013.

3. Scahill, J. Dirty Wars: The World Is A Battlefield. Nation Books, 2013.

4. Chossudovsky, M. The Globalization of War, America's "Long War" against Humanity. Global Research, 2015.

5. Benjamin, M. Drone Warfare: Killing by Remote Control. Verso, 2013.

6. Cohen, M. (Ed.). Drones and Targeted Killing: Legal, Moral, and Geopolitical Issues. Olive Branch Press, February 3, 2015.

7. Eisler, R. The Real Wealth of Nations: Creating a Caring Economics. San Francisco: Berrett-Koehler, 2007; The Chalice and the Blade: Our History, Our Future. Harper One, 1988.

8. Zinn, H. A People's History of the United States. Harper Perennial, 2005 (first published in 1980).

9. Greeley, B. Harley Rider Mitch Daniels Was Afraid of Howard Zinn. Bloomberg Businessweek, July 17, 2013.

10. For some studies and accounts of the varnishing of American history in education and in public disseminations generally see, e.g., Fitzgerald, F. America Revised: History Schoolbooks in the Twentieth Century. Little Brown and Co., 1979; Loewen, JW. Lies My Teacher Told Me: Everything Your American History Textbook Got Wrong. New Press, 2008; and Cohn, M. US Government Sanitizes Vietnam War History. Global Research, October 30, 2014.

CHAPTER 1
UNBROKEN HABITS

America is addicted to two chronic and costly habits, warring and spying. The two are neither unique to America nor to this time in history. They originated when civilization originated, yet for some time the American version has been unparalleled throughout the world. The two are different in that warring takes away lives and spying takes away privacy and freedom. Yet the two go hand in hand. Both need enemies. In America, the habits began when America began. Let's start with the more costly habit of warring.

Brief History of America's Unbroken War Habit

America was born in the womb of war and since her birth has never known a significant interlude when there were no overt or covert wars or the preparing for them.

Gestated in War

Before she was even born America had become addicted to the warring habit. The colonists, wanting the land occupied by the Native Americans already there waged war against these people. This was a dress rehearsal for what was to become inevitable, a new nation that over time would muscle its way through wars and other military interventions into becoming the world's dominant market force, superpower, and rogue nation.

Born in the Womb of War

The costly American Revolution, started by the colonists who were not loyal to the King, gave birth to America. It was an unnecessary war. To be sure, the colonists presented King George a long list of grievances in their Declaration of Independence, but by signing it they had no intention of relying on state craft to seek a nonviolent resolution. Their "olive branch" petition sent later to the King, moreover, was clearly insincere and the King knew it, since he got it after he was sent the Declaration of Independence. [1]

The Founding Fathers were clearly in no mood for reconciliation. They were already creatures of habit and heritage. Most descended from England, a belligerent and imperialistic country that "during its history---invaded, had some control over, or fought conflicts in 171 of the world's 193 countries that are currently UN member states, or nine out of ten of all countries." [2] In the 18th century alone the "Mother Country" was embroiled in 15 wars prior to the American Revolution. [3]

Seeking a settlement with "Mad King George" would not have been as ludicrous as it may seem. His troops, fighting far away on foreign soil would never have prevailed in the long run, nor would have his colonial empire. It would have eventually expired from exhaustion, lack of resources, and sense of futility. The American Revolution was a Pyrrhic victory for the revolutionaries, leaving over 25,000 of them dead and as many wounded and predisposing the new nation to a future of warring as a solution to conflicts and as a means to further its own colonizing. [4]

2

One of the most influential persons of that period was Thomas Paine. His pamphlet, "Common Sense," is credited with having "galvanized" the colonists into fighting the war and in imbuing in them a sense of America's exceptional nature as a new country of unlimited opportunity. [5] He ought to be credited instead with helping to sow more seeds conceptually for America's chronic war habit. There was nothing "common sense" about losing so many lives that could have been avoided, and his parochial and arrogant thinking about America being special would evolve into the idea of America's "manifest destiny," coined by an American columnist, editor, and political appointee in 1845 that has served as an ideology and rationale frequently used by America's leaders to justify her militaristic imperialism. [6]

The Critical Period

The period between the end of the American Revolution in 1783 and the inauguration of the nation's first president, George Washington in 1789 has been called the "critical period" because America was a new nation in name only. [7] The 13 states were at each other's throats figuratively speaking and largely over land acquisition.

This critical period should also be called the "unduplicated period" because it is the only period in the history of America as a nation where she was not at war, planning war, or carrying out clandestine and hostile operations of one sort or another in one place or another to this day and still with no end in sight.

The critical period was also the time in which the U.S. Constitution was written and then ratified in 1788-1789. It is appropriate here to take a brief and iconoclastic look at that revered blueprint and its framers because their document and their experience in the Revolutionary War and the ubiquity of war in the old country indirectly influenced the beginnings of America's chronic war habit. War was customary and it would become that way too in the new nation.

The framers did not really mean or intend to fulfill the high-sounding principles in the Constitution. They were a morally deficient group of plutocrats who favored the propertied elite and had no intention of allowing a genuine democracy that would have given equal representation to the unwashed masses. What happened instead was exactly what was intended to happen; for example, indentured servants fleeing from one State to another were required to be returned to their masters; slaves were treated as not fully human and slavery as an economically acceptable means of exploiting them; no mention was made in the Constitution of accommodating the Indian Nation already on the continent that would soon be destroyed by the new government's expansionism; and while stating in the document's preamble the purpose of providing for the common defense the framers then proceeded to provide for the declaration of war without specifying any conditions (other than duration of funding) and without preferring and promoting diplomatic means of defense by settling disputes among nations. [8]

In short, by not creating a blueprint for a truly egalitarian, socially responsible and peaceful nation guided by universal albeit sporadically practiced ethical values the framers designed a nation for people like them and squandered the opportunity to make the "world's first new nation" a truly exemplary model of civilization.

America's First Warrior-in-Chief

As the nation's first president George Washington also became the nation's first "warrior-in-chief." He advocated a "regular and standing" army to "awe the Indians, protect our Trade, prevent the encroachment of our Neighbours of Canada and the Florida's---[and] establishing arsenals of all kinds of military stores." [9] He relied on that army in the Northwest Indian War that resulted in several thousand casualties and also in quelling the so-called "whiskey rebellion." [10] Why should any different behavior have been expected from a man who was an experienced warrior on numerous occasions even before the American Revolution? [11]

After George Washington

After George Washington left office America continued being a warrior nation without missing a heartbeat except for just two occasions when the hearts of two presidents stopped beating shortly after entering office in the 19th century. Since his time the U.S. government has built a massive war bureaucracy, once honestly and officially known as the Department of War before being renamed in 1949 the Department of Defense.

Since his time America has engaged in declared and undeclared wars 11 times and has conducted approximately 13,000 to 14,000 other overt and covert military interventions and there is no sign or little chance of them stopping anytime soon. [12] Hardly a spot on the globe has been untouched by the terror of and casualties from America's show of force. After reviewing America's militarism, Noam Chomsky, emeritus professor at the Massachusetts Institute of Technology, concluded that the U.S. "is the world's leading terrorist state." [13]

I need to mention USSOCOM before moving on. Does it draw a blank with you? It certainly is not a garden variety acronym. It stands for the U.S. Special Operations Command that conducts secret operations/wars.

I have Nick Turse, managing editor of Tomdispatch.com and an Investigative Fund Fellow at The Nation Institute to thank for educating me about it. He reports that USSOCOM has implanted operations, or "secret wars" in 134 countries, or nearly 70% of the world's sovereign states. He writes prosaically that "They operate in the green glow of night vision in Southwest Asia and stalk through the jungles of South America. They snatch men from their homes in the Maghreb and shoot it out with heavily armed militants in the Horn of Africa. They feel the salty spray while skimming over the tops of waves from the turquoise Caribbean to the deep blue Pacific. They conduct missions in the oppressive heat of Middle Eastern deserts and the deep freeze of Scandinavia." [14] Mr. Turse's article drew this cogent comment from a reader, "As a former U.S. ambassador to Canada once put it: "The US doesn't have friends. It has interests." [15]

The Birth of the War on Terror

The tragic attack on American soil by foreign terrorists on September 11, 2001 gave birth to the "war on terror" and has proven to be a boon for the war and spy enterprise. According to Dr. Paul Craig Roberts, an official in the Reagan Administration, editor, columnist, and book author, the war on terror is a "hoax:" "If America were infected with terrorists," he wrote, "we would not need the government to tell us. We would know it from events. As there are no events, the US government substitutes warnings in order to keep alive the fear that causes the public to accept pointless wars." [16] He wrote his article before the Boston Marathon bombing but his point has a grain of truth about it. America is not being invaded by a swarm of terrorists; there is no indication of any pending invasion; and the bungling intelligence community would probably fail to see it coming in any case. A similar point made after that bombing is that the war on terror is a fabrication concocted to defend America's police state. [17]

My own opinion is that the war on terror is overblown in scale and intensity. There is, goodness knows, the potential for terrorism directed again at the U.S. and emanating from anywhere among the many countries where the U.S. has conducted military and intelligence operations just in this 21st century. While the only sure way to stop or minimize terrorist attacks would be for the U.S. to stop terrorizing and bullying other countries, moderate rather than wholesale and illegal forms of vigilance by the U.S. ought to be sufficient. But, of course, the war and spy business has no sense of moderation, just the taste of money and power. And that is why the U.S. does not negotiate with terrorist groups, yet negotiating with them, believe it or not, has been found to work better than fighting them. [18]

Brief History of America's Unbroken Spying Habit

Besides being America's first warrior-in-chief, George Washington was her first chief spy. His and his agents' spying on the British forces were instrumental in the defeat of them. As president, he asked Congress to fund his "Secret Service Fund." The authorization grew from $40,000 the first year to $1 million within just three years, which amounted to about 12% of the entire U.S. budget. [19]

Unlike the history of her war habit in both its overt and covert forms that never had a lengthy pause or a defining moment, America's spying was relatively episodic and accompanied by almost countless reorganizations along with three defining moments that led to significant expansion. The first was WWII. The second was the Cold War, which, until the third defining moment was credited with giving the biggest boost to the whole spying enterprise. The third, of course, was the already mentioned terrorist attack of September 11, 2001 on America's homeland, which was an absolute bonanza for the spy enterprise and gave the spy agencies and the White House along with cooperative local law enforcement the excuse to turn America into a police state that unlawfully:

> Arrests peaceful protestors
> Inhibits constitutionally protected dissent
> Builds a huge, ridiculously costly citizens'
> "metadata" store house in Utah
> Maintains data on over one million
> Americans
> Conducts warrantless searches
> Forcefully enters homes with falsified
> warrants
> Considers using drone surveillance in
> America
> Uses the sinister sounding and really
> sinister
> "disposition matrix"
> Detains citizens without trial
> Established an extra judicial court to rubber
> stamp spy activities
> Intimidates the not-free press
> Issues "National Security Letters forcing
> release of customer records

Misuses the already illegal Patriot Act
Monitors Americans' private
communications
Targets for killing Americans suspected of
being terrorists
Traces and builds citizens' "friend-of-
friend" networks
Uses cryptic spy tools like "PRISM" and
Boundless Informant"
Uses secret evidence and witnesses in trials
Uses small aircraft to trick cell phones to
reveal messages
And whatever else [20]

Naturally the chief spies, and there are many spy agencies to be chiefs of (see Chapter 4), will not admit even under oath that their agencies are monitoring Americans, collecting, analyzing, and storing the mountains of data collected. The Defense Intelligence Chief, for instance, reportedly lied when directly asked in an open Congressional hearing whether NSA was spying on American citizens. [21] It didn't matter though. The committee members knew the truth but weren't about to charge the chief with perjury because they themselves are complicit in the spy business since their political careers benefit from the spy industry's campaign financing. [22]

Yet keeping massive secrets is hard to keep secret when there are thousands of people in the spy community with access to spy data. Just a few months after that testimony, for instance, truth got a measure of revenge when Edward Snowden left his job with a NSA contractor, taking with him 1.7 million classified documents and started leaking them [23]
Occasionally truth has a friend who is not a chief spy but is a senior level spy official. Jim Fetzer, a former Marine

Corps officer and subsequently Professor Emeritus at the University of Minnesota, wrote in an article that a "top official" stated that, "Everybody's a target; everybody with communication is a target."[24] Even if that candid statement was made "without attribution," it was still made.

Occasionally there is a slip of the tongue or a real gaffe and the truth spills out as it did on Andrea Mitchell's NBC Nightly News, January 17, 2014 when Michael Hayden, a retired general and former director of both the CIA and NSA, was seen and heard saying: "We aren't out there hoovering (sic) everything in the universe up for some prurient interest. We are gathering data to make America more profitable for more commercial enterprises." [25]

In other words, Mr. Hayden, you are admitting that the real purpose of NSA and presumably the rest of the national intelligence enterprise is to make American corporations more profitable by helping out in doing corporate espionage work. Mr. Hayden should be complimented for his revelation and severely punished for his conduct.

But there's also another real purpose of official spying, one about which Mr. Hayden is more tightlipped, the intimidation and control of Americans by gathering data on them. Domestic spying is a key tool of a police state. Freedom of speech and freedom to dissent, two Constitutional rights, have turned into fear of speaking out and dissenting against officialdom.

The American Branch of Homo Sapiens

The history of America we have just read spans only 238 years, a mere speck of time. Our species began about

200,000 years ago and started recording its history probably first by wall paintings about 35,000 years ago. As far as I know, our species along with the ant species and possibly our DNA cousins the chimps are the only species that wage war on their own kind. Members of our species have evolved increasingly sophistical means of killing one another, with the American Branch probably being the most technologically advanced killer. That it does not behead its own members, and ever since the Donner Pass episode in 1846-1847 no longer cannibalizes its own members, is hardly a sign of progress in its humanness since it probably holds the world record in killing human beings and is responsible for the savagery and perversity of the CIA's torture program. [26]

Endnotes

1. Wikipedia. Olive Branch Petition.
2. Wikipedia. List of Wars Involving England.
3. Wikipedia. American Revolution
4. Wikipedia. United States Military Casualties of War
5. Wikipedia. Common Sense.
6. See, e.g., Greenwald, G. The Premises And Purposes Of American Exceptionalism OpEdNews February 18, 2013; Lubragge, MT. Manifest Destiny - The Philosophy That Created A Nation. University of Groningen, The Netherlands, August, 2012; Wikipedia. American Exceptionalsim; and Wikipedia. John L. O'Sullivan.
7.The American History Company. The Critical Period, 1783-1789. www.americanhistory.com
8. Zinn, H. A People's History of the United States. Harper Perennial, 2005 (first published in 1980).
9. Wikipedia. George Washington. See also; George Washington, Sentiments on a Peace Establishment. May 2, 1783.
10. Wikipedia. Shay's Rebellion.

11. Wikipedia. Military Career of George Washington.

12. The U.S. government is not about to publish a detailed, official list of its overt and covert military operations since the American Revolution. Any tabulation of these operations, therefore, depends on digging up finding out about them from other sources such as these two sources: Ridenour, R. Born in the USA Regimen of Permanent Wars. Counterpunch, December 25, 2012; Wilson, S.B. History US military Overt and Covert Global Interventions July 15, 2012. /www.brianwillson.com

13. Chomsky, N. Noam Chomsky: The Leading Terrorist State. Truthout, November 3, 2014.

14. Turse, N. America's Secret War in 134 Countries. The Nation, January 16, 2014

15. A Mr. Terry Lawrence posted the comment in The Nation, January 17, 2014.

16. Roberts, PC. The War on Terror is a Hoax. OpEdNews, February 4, 2009.

17. Petras, J. The Obama Regime's Fabricated "Terror Conspiracy" in Defense of the Police State. Global Research, August 14, 2013.

18. Rand Corporation. How Terrorist Groups End: Implications for Countering al Qa'ida. Rand Research Brief RB935, 2008.

19. Two authoritative sources on the history of America's foreign and domestic spying are these: Federation of Scientists. The Evolution of the U.S. Intelligence Community-An Historical Overview. Undated. http://www.fas.org/irp/budget/index.html; and McCoy, A. It's About Blackmail, Not National Security. TomDispatch.com, January 19, 2014.

20. See e.g., these selected sources: Butigan, K. Challenging the 'Disposition Matrix' and its Ever-expanding Kill List. Waging Nonviolence, November 1, 2012; Calamur, K. 5 Things To Know About The NSA's Surveillance Activities, NPR, October 23, 2013; Cushing,

The NSA Turns Everyone Into A 'Threat To National Security By Instantly Classifying All Data It Scoops Up. Truthdig, July 8, 2013, www.techdirt.com; Gentile, S. Are We Becoming a Police State? Five Things That Have Civil Liberties Advocates Nervous. The Daily Need, December 7, 2011; Greenwald, G. NSA Collecting Phone Records of Millions of Verizon Customers Daily. The Guardian, June 5, 2013; Hill, K. Blueprints Of NSA's Ridiculously Expensive Data Center In Utah Suggest It Holds Less Info Than Thought. Forbes, July 24, 2013; Hiken, M. & Hiken, L. Police in the U.S. are an Invading Army. Dissident Voice, September 11, 2012; Hirthler, J. Bonfire of the Liberties. Dissident Voice, January 16, 2013; Jacobsen, K. NSA Revelations: A Timeline of What's Come Out Since Snowden Leaks Began. Christian Science Monitor, June 5-8, 2013; McCombs, B. NSA's Utah Home Is A 1.5 Million Square Foot 'Spy Center. AP, June 6, 2013; Queally, J. Revealed: US Agency Using Spy Planes to Fool Cell Phones, Capture Data. Cyrano's Journal, November 16, 2014; Roberts, PC. It Has Happened Here. OpEdNews, February 7, 2013; and Van Buren, P. You Can't Opt Out 10 NSA Myths Debunked. TomDispatch.com, January 12, 2014.

21. Kaplan, F. Fire James Clapper. Slate Magazine, June 11, 2013.

22. Shaw, D. Intelligence Contractors Give Millions to Lawmakers Overseeing Government Surveillance. Map Light, December 7, 2013.

23. Kelley, M. NSA: Snowden Stole 1.7 Million Classified Documents And Still Has Access To Most Of Them . Business Insider, December 13, 2013.

24. Fetzer, J. US Terror Alert a Political Stunt and Other American NSA Absurdities. Veterans Today, August 6, 2013.

25. Wolf, R. What IS the Purpose of the NSA? Cyrano's Journal, January 21, 2014. You can hear this by following

this link: www.cjournal.info/2014/01/21/what-is-the-purpose-of-the-nsa

26. 26. See, .e.g., Chossudovsky, M. The Role of 9/11 in Justifying Torture and War: The Criminalization of the US State Apparatus. Senate Report on CIA Torture is a Whitewash. Global Research, December 11, 2014; Volsky, I.17 Disgraceful Facts Buried In The Senate's 600 Page Torture Report. Think Progress, December 9, 2014; and Wolf, R. Read the Investigation of the CIA "Detention" and "Interrogation" Programs for Yourself. Cyrano's Journal, December 10, 2014.

CHAPTER 2
COSTLY HABITS

America's two habits are clearly no ordinary ones. Ordinary ones range from harmless indulgence to expensive and harmful addictions. America's two habits have much fewer manifestations, but all go far beyond self-indulgence, typically are dreadfully consequential in monetary and human costs, and usually affect not just individuals but also the socioeconomic and political conditions of entire nations, with the U.S. invasion of Iraq being a recent example, not to mention the adverse effects on all elements of America's society.

The Human Costs, Statistically Speaking

Over two and one-half million Americans have been sent to their graves from military interventions authorized by America's warriors-in-chief. [1] The most deadly internal war, the Civil War, sent over 600 thousand Americans to their graves. Add to all of the foregoing blood spilling the six to seven million civilians who died from U.S. military intervention in Korea, Vietnam, and Iraq. Add to that a former CIA agent's estimate that six million people have died from covert CIA operations alone. Then add the mounting death toll from President Barack Obama's drone killings by the thousands in far-away places like Afghanistan, Algeria, Iraq, Iran, Libya, Pakistan, Yemen, Somalia and probably more that are still secret. [2] Based on his exhaustive study, James Lucas, a retired social worker and currently an anti-war activist and writer, estimates that U.S. military interventions have been directly responsible for between 20 and 30 million civilian deaths throughout 37 countries just since after WWII and only up to 2007. [3]

An incredulous fact (until you know the facts) about America's wars and all other wars throughout history is that 50% or more of the casualties have been non-combatants, and this casualty rate figure soared to 85% during America's invasion of Iraq. [4] With the advent of

46

President Obama's drone strikes that kill maybe a few potential terrorists and hundreds of innocent civilians, including children, that rate is probably around 100%, a fact not too hard to believe at all since the strikes apparently seldom hit confirmed combatants . Conclusion? Wars don't liberate civilians. Wars kill them.

To the casualties and human suffering from America's use of force must also be added the human suffering from America's use of sanctions to bring countries to their knees. In an admission that would be indictable as an international war crime if not made by American officials, in this case Vice President Joe Biden and outgoing Secretary of State Hillary Clinton, "both openly admitted that the U.S.-led sanctions against Iran (and Syria) are politically motivated and constitute a "soft-war" against the nearly 80 million people of Iran (23 million people in Syria) in order to achieve regime change." [5] The administration's claim that there are no sanctions on medicine, food, and other necessities belies the known fact that multinational corporations are reluctant to ship supplies to a sanctioned country for fear of violating a bureaucratic technicality.

In what must be one of the most morally offensive remarks by a U.S. official was the televised answer by Secretary of State Madeleine Albright to reporter Lesley Stahl's question about whether the price of sanctions against Iran were worth it considering half a million children died as a result. "I think this is a very hard choice, but the price--we think the price is worth it," the Secretary of State answered. [6] What choice did the children have, Madam Albright?

The Human Costs, Human Beings' Speaking

> Dead men by mass production—in one
> country after another —month after month
> and year after year. To you at home
> they are columns of figures, or he is a near
> one who went away and just didn't come
> back. You didn't see him lying so
> grotesque and pasty beside the gravel road
> in France. We saw him, saw him by the
> multiple thousands.
> That's the difference.
>
> ---Ernie Pyle

Those were the posthumous sentiments of the WWII correspondent Ernie Pyle. [7] He was acknowledging a simple truth about human nature. Numbers about humanity cannot speak to humanity like human beings can. As Mr. Pyle knew, even tabulations of horrific consequences of war tend to numb and depersonalize reactions to them (with the exception of the casualties on America's home land, September 11, 2001). Adding personal stories like the few selected below ought to help elicit some form of emotional response at least to all but the most hardened and insensitive of people, including sociopaths (who may be overrepresented among America's warriors and spies).

Michael Moore, Oscar, Emmy and book award winner collected and published letters from soldiers in Iraq and their families back home. The following vignette is from one of those letters. [8]

> *---my son was killed in Iraq---. He was*
> *going to be a proud father of a baby boy. --*
> *-the Army would not pay for us to go to his*
> *funeral. Several months later they*
> *offered to fly us free to meet with*

President Bush. No thanks.

Not all deaths happen on the battlefield. Many soldiers who escape death there meet it back home by their own means. According to a Veterans Affairs report a veteran commits suicide every 80 minutes. It is the final stage of what clinicians call "post-traumatic stress syndrome." A case in point among thousands is the late William Busbee, who was in the Army Special Forces, airborne and the Army Rangers. [9]

> ---Mr. Busbee *"sat with a .45-caliber gun pointed to the side of his head. 'Look at me,' his mother cried out as she tried to get her son's attention. 'Look at me. Don't you do this. Don't do it. He wouldn't turn his head to look at me.' [Then he] took his life---with his mother and sister looking on.*

> *He told me how he picked up the body parts and loaded them onto a helicopter so their families would have something to bury, his mother said. She said her son had tried to commit suicide in Pesh Valley of Afghanistan. He told me, Momma, the William you knew died over there.*

Like the legendary Mafia don with his hit list or like a "one-man death panel," Nobel Peace Laureate Barack Obama sits in his office and picks people from the drone hit list handed to him by his chief terrorism advisor. [10] Later, people thousands of miles away get hit. Thousands have been hit and killed so far. Among them are innocents not connected to any terrorist group who the killers euphemistically refer to as "collateral damage."

Sometimes the dead were elders riding in a bus to a village meeting to resolve a community issue having nothing to with America. [11]

> ---the loss of 40 leaders on a single day is
> devastating for that community---the strike
> actually removed, in one fell swoop,
> the most stabilizing forces in an entire
> community. A nearby villager remembers
> the attack, which also claimed four of his
> cousins. The villager's six-year-old son was
> later afraid – to sleep in their house, saying
> We cannot go home. We have to spend the
> night in the tree.

Sometimes the dead were more than a dozen members of a wedding party. [12]

> Scorched vehicles and body parts were left
> scattered on the road.

"Bride and Boom" headlined the insensitive New York Post, referring to that scene in Yemen. From an entirely different perspective, one of humaneness and disgust was the comment by Tom Engelhardt, journalist, editor, book author, and university instructor that "'Till death do us part' has gained a far grimmer meaning." [13]

Sometimes the dead were beloved grandmothers. [14]

> ---a father with his two children—came all
> the way from the Pakistani tribal territory
> of North Waziristan to the US Capitol
> to tell the heart-wrenching story of the
> death of the children's beloved 67-year-old
> grandmother. Watching the beautiful 9-

50

year-old Nabila relate how her
grandmother was blown to bits while
outside picking okra softened the hearts of
even the most hardened DC politicos.

That last scene was depicted in an article by Medea Benjamin, book author and staunch critic of war and drone strikes. While I respect her eyewitness account, I doubt that "the hearts of most hardened DC politicos" were softened because she reports that only five members of Congress attended the hearings. [15] That leaves out over 500 more hardened politicos who didn't bother to attend it.

Sometimes the dead from drone strikes were children, several hundred so far; among them infants of 1, 2, 3 and 4 years old; sometimes the dead were brothers and sisters of an entire family. [16]

Four sisters, ages 4 to 9 years were struck
and killed by an American drone strike.
Four children, ages 3 to 13 years old
in a different family in the same country
were struck and killed by an American
drone strike.

Pause for a moment and ask yourself this question: What kind of a human being is it in the Oval Office that authorizes these deadly strikes?

Drone strikes, of course, are just the newest technological age of U.S. barbarism that kills people, among them children. It's an old story, with just the technology having changed.

Margaret Kimberley, a New York based writer and activist for peace and justice issues notes that "America has a long history of killing little children. Hundreds of thousands of children were taken from Africa to be enslaved in America, little children were lynching victims and children are now killed by drones, sanctions, and the other aggressions that this country meets out to the rest of the world."

She estimates that "the number of children killed by American militarism and covert wars since WWII is easily in the order of 20 million." [17] I have no idea how much of these 20 million children are included in the estimate of 20 to 30 million civilian deaths cited earlier.

But does a more precise estimate really matter? Children of the world, at the mercy of stronger and older people, are meant to be loved and nourished, not murdered.

President Obama: Sickening---Sickening--- Sickening. I can't say it enough times.

Another sickening form of America's war habit is the practice of torturing captives. Torture sometimes amounts to death cruelly delayed. The U.S. reportedly has authorized torture chambers in more than 54 countries, a revelation that "should make all of us in this country cringe with shame." [18]. How are people, judged guilty by the torturers, actually tortured? Think about a U.S. regime that relies on torture to try and extract confessions and information from human beings held captive in "black sites, borrowed prisons and by borrowed torturers in many cases" [19]. Think about an American regime that approves of treating human beings like this:

> Can't sit, stand or lie down
> Beaten, excruciating pain, testicles whipped
> Deprived of sleep

Given inadequate food and water
Hooded
Humiliated
Jammed into small boxes
Naked
Shackled
Slammed into walls
Sodomized
Water poured into mouth and lungs

Peter Van Buren, a 24-year veteran Foreign Service Officer (since retired) at the State Department, has pointed out that "Horrific as it may be, pain fades, bones mend, bruises heal. No, don't for a second think that the essence of torture is physical pain. If, in many cases, the body heals, mental wounds are a far more difficult matter. Memory persists." That is especially so, he points out, with the victim's sense of humiliation from being so helpless. [20]

Other Non-Monetary Costs

We should probably stop right here for a moment and mourn the lives lost, the lives maimed, the lives of those with lost loved ones, and the lives of those with lives altered in other devastating ways, all of whom the leaders of America's corpocracy sacrificed for their own self-interest. It almost seems callous to say there are other "costs." But there are. There are many more. And we must not ignore them for the incalculable damage they have done and are doing to America and Americans. The "people's court" needs to know how much to hold the regimes' accountable, at least symbolically, for their crimes and other wrongdoing because the regimes so far have managed to stay above the law and avoid being held accountable.

Environmental Degradation

I am considering environmental degradation to be a non-monetary cost because it is impossible to put a price tag on it.

America's military not only kills people, it kills the environment. In the Vietnam War, for instance, the chemical Agent Orange was used to defoliate the countryside so as to better see the enemy. That was an instance of deliberate destruction of the environment. Most of the military's destruction is a byproduct of military operations.

One of the biggest polluters is the Department of Defense. [21] Here is a sample of DOD's destructive imprint on the environment:

> Abandoned waste at military bases dotting the globe
> Defoliation and desertification
> Depleted uranium
> Insatiable use of fossil fuels
> Land mines and cluster bombs left behind
> Toxic contamination of the air
> Toxic contamination of resources for drinking water
> Toxic contamination of soil

If Armageddon ever comes there will be no livable planet and no living human beings.

The Loss of Privacy, Freedom, and a Shrinking Liberty Quotient

Americans have lost their Constitutional right to privacy and live in the land of the watched. "We have no place to hide" exclaims Robert Scheer, distinguished journalist and prolific book author. [22] Neither, apparently, do leaders of foreign countries spied on by America's international spying ring. [23]

In a warfare and police state its citizens are not really citizens in a democracy. They are subjects in a corpocracy, the collusion between government and big corporations, including those in the war and spy industries, with government in a subservient role. Citizens living in a corpocracy   have lost their freedom as citizens to live their own lives within socially appropriate and legal boundaries.

Marcus Tullius Cicero, the Roman Consul and Orator (106BC-43BC), said that freedom is participation in power. Cicero, who wrote Western civilization's first democratic constitution, prized freedom. In one of his presidential campaign messages Ralph Nader noted that by Cicero's definition "freedom is in short supply for tens of millions of Americans."[24] Since then the supply is nearly non-existent for all powerless Americans, which is about 99% of Americans.

The reason Cicero believed freedom is participation in power is because power means control and a free people in a true democracy have more rather than less control over whether and how much health, happiness, and prosperity they have. Think of a "liberty quotient" that gauges one's personal freedom as a ratio of freedom over subjugation. Now compare the liberty quotient of a plutocrat with that of an average wage earner or a homeless person.

So the notion of freedom, or our liberty quotient, is tied inexorably to power and control over our lives, absolutely every sphere of it, whether the personal/social/cultural sphere, the economic sphere, the political sphere, or the environmental sphere. [25]

Benjamin Franklin said it best: "Those who would give up essential liberty to purchase a little temporary safety deserve neither."

The Lost Opportunity to Achieve Peace

This is the most serious loss. Unless peace can be achieved America will remain a warfare and police state with all the risks it entails, including the unthinkable, Armageddon (see Chapter 8).

The Lost Opportunity to Rebuild America

Trillions of dollars over the years have been wasted on America's two habits. Just since 1948 over 20 trillion dollars reportedly has been spent on the military budget. [26] I once estimated that one-half of that amount is sheer "warfare welfare," the other half reflecting a realistic defense budget limited to the costs of responding to attacks on our shores by foreign states and terrorist groups. That amounts to least over 10 trillion dollars in lost opportunity costs since 1948. [27]

Money squandered on habits is money spent that is no longer available for useful expenditures. It's money that could have been spent over more than a 60-year period on meeting pressing domestic and global needs in employment, education, nutrition, health care, sanitation, you name it.

By losing this opportunity America has become the worst among industrialized nations in income inequality, unemployment rate, food insecurity, life expectancy at birth, and prison population. America is a country in which four of five U.S. adults struggle with joblessness, near-poverty or reliance on welfare for at least parts of their lives; a country in which one million public school students are homeless and over 16 million live in poverty; a country in which thousands upon thousands of homeless people live in tunnels beneath the streets of major U.S. cities. [28] Such are the "sadtistics" about America.

Had we not lost the opportunity, had our government, as prescribed in the Constitution provided for the general welfare and not the welfare of the corpocracy, including its warriors and spies, America would be a very different America today, an educated America, an employed America, a healthy America, a happy America, and an America at peace with the world.

The War Resisters League has given us some tabulated examples of what could have been done constructively with the money spent just on the Iraq war: "48,801,253 children could have attended a year of Head Start; we could have built 3,317,543 additional housing units for low-income people; we could have hired 6,385,283 additional public school teachers for one year; or provided 17,861,650 students four-year scholarships at public universities---." [29] And I will add that had peace broken out all over after the initial Iraq War, we could have spent the war money saved from then through now for more research to find cures for cancer and Alzheimer's, for rebuilding bridges so cars don't crash into the water and sink, for ending water and air pollutions, for ending poverty once and for all, and for getting closer to the Alter America that is envisioned in Chapter 7.

The Erosion of Civil Standards and the Unraveling of Society

In times of war, the law falls silent.
---Cicero 106BC-43BC

Civil standards are guidelines and requirements for how to behave in a civilized society so that it remains a civilized society. There are two kinds of standards, the universal ethical or moral values that are the guidelines and the rule of law that are the requirements.

Universal moral or ethical values are the highest standard because, as the saying goes, morality can't be legislated. Countless laws would be needed to do so. There are just too many ways to breech the different values (namely; accountability, caring for others, excellence, fairness, honesty, integrity, justice, loyalty, promise keeping, respecting others, and responsibility) that a lawyer turned ethicist, an unusual twist, found in his search for them across centuries and cultures. [30].

These values are independent of any religious beliefs. They are, in short, humanity's universal values. They matter because violating them has harmful consequences of some kind (whether financial, psychological, and/or physical) and degree (from trivial to deadly). The earliest humans noticed those consequences and that explains how the values became universal and timeless. You will see as we go along in this book that it is an account of these values being persistently and egregiously breached, more so than in any time in history.

Any nation is both morally and legally bound to honor the lower standard, the rule of law. There are two rules of law that must not be violated by any nation, domestic law and international law. America's leaders have consistently violated both. According to Frances Boyle, an authority on international law, "more than 30 top U.S. officials, including presidents G.W. Bush and Obama, are guilty of war crimes or crimes against peace and humanity" legally akin to those perpetrated by the former Nazi regime in Germany. [31]

Here are some of those laws:

First, Fourth, Fifth, Sixth, and Eight Amendments
Foreign Intelligence Surveillance Act
Geneva Convention's Article 3
Rome Statute (Article 7) of the International Criminal Court
UN Charter's Articles 2, 5, 33, and 51
U.S. Constitution Articles 1 and 3
Whistleblower protection laws

If these two sets of standards were ever to be completely eroded America's society would unravel, and not coincidentally we are now witnessing the early stages of America unraveling. [32] A more dire prediction, namely, that we are headed toward WWWIII or the "final war" is being increasingly made by authoritative sources. [33]

The conventional argument is that there is a difference between "just" and "unjust" wars. It's the argument that helps people addicted to or tolerant of the war habit to rationalize it, to make it seem acceptable that millions of people have died at the first, second, and more hands of Americans. An alternative argument, which I expand upon in Appendix A, is that there is no such thing as a "just" or even necessary war.

And any and all laws against murder

Albert Einstein, one of the greatest thinkers of all times, made a succinct argument against war. "It is my conviction," he once said, "that killing under the cloak of war is nothing but an act of murder." For an intellectual, he was extremely emotional about it, as he also said, "I would rather be torn to shreds than be a part of so base an action!" [34]

If Einstein's argument is valid and irrefutable, as I think and argue in Appendix A that it is, then an inescapable but highly uncomfortable conclusion is that agents that do the actual killing in war are murderers and agents that authorize, order and provide the means of war are surrogate murderers. That is a conclusion I am sure most Americans would not care to embrace, which is one reason why America's war habit has not been broken.

Twisted Loyalty and Patriotism

Loyalty can be good, bad, or false. Good loyalty can be expressed as a plea by truly patriotic citizens, "My country, please do right and no wrong." Jingoistic patriotism, or "my country right or wrong," is bad loyalty. It is the kind that helped sustain Hitler's brutal regime and killing machine. Jingoistic patriotism is fueled by demagogues and war mongers for self-serving interests.

The Loss of Truth

"Not a single thing that we commonly believe about wars that helps keep them around is true," says David Swanson, author and antiwar activist. [35] In a warfare and police state truth is hidden by the state and by its allies such as the mainstream media (See Chapter 6). The state doesn't dare tell the truth about its warring and spying for fear of provoking and succumbing to public backlash.

Lincoln Caplan, a member of The American Scholar's editorial board wrote recently in that journal asking whether journalists who leak state secrets are "leakers or traitors." The government's answer he says, that they are traitors, puts "a free press at risk." [36] No one knows that risk better than the leakers and the whistleblowers who feed the journalists the state's secrets.

State secrets are meant to protect the security of the regime, not to protect the freedom of the people subjugated by the regime. The makers and keepers of state secrets are the traitors, not the leakers of those secrets. As columnist Frank Rich once said, "---if there's to be a witch hunt for traitors, the top of our government is where it should begin, [with] the real traitors,---the officials who squandered American blood and treasure on an ill-considered (Iraq) war and then tried to cover up their lies and mistakes." [37]

Recall the story about one of the chief spies allegedly lying in a public testimony before Congress. Here's another story. The article about it started off with a picture. Shown were five white men properly suited and seated and answering questions at a Congressional hearing: the National Counterterrorism Center Director, the FBI Director, Director of National Intelligence (yes, the same one in the first story), the CIA Director, and the Defense Intelligence Agency Director.

That's a whopping lot of spy chiefs at one table, and according to Paul Craig Roberts, the author of the article, they were traitors telling Congress whopping lies. "Congress," the author wrote, "is content to sit there and listen to their ongoing lies time after time after time, despite the fact that these 5 have committed more and worse crimes against our country than the "terrorists" that serve as an excuse for the crimes committed by the intelligence agencies." [38]

The Loss of Trust

Trust is having confidence that people, organizations and institutions will do what they should do. Critics of America's two addictions obviously have no trust in their government to stop its warring and spying.

Trust takes on a different twist in the spook business. Spooks trust other spooks on the same side to keep their secrets. Spooks who are double agents walk a fine line of trust, not being overly confident about which side to trust. The height of double spooking was probably the Cold War era, a childish but dangerous conflict. Malcolm Gladwell, prolific book author and critic-at-large at The New Yorker has written a spellbinding review of a spellbinding book about double agent Kim Philby during the Cold War. I mention this article because Gladwell makes a point I want to extend. He comments that few spy secrets are of any strategic value. [39] Precisely, Mr. Gladwell; spying epitomizes what we psychologists call "functional autonomy," and in this case it is exemplified by spying for the sake of spying.

Blowback

Blowback is an extreme form of what I call "boomerang harm." The deadly "9/11" al-Qaeda terrorist air strikes on the Twin Towers, the Pentagon and the deliberate crash of another passenger plane were heinous, punishable acts, no doubt about it, but they were also blowback by people seeking to settle a score for America's skewed foreign policy, imperialism, heavy military presence, and covert and overt deadly interventions in the Greater Middle East. In his November 2002 Letter to America, "Osama bin Laden explicitly stated that al-Qaeda's motives for their attacks included Western support for attacking Muslims in Somalia, supporting Russian atrocities against Muslims in Chechnya, supporting the Indian oppression against Muslims in Kashmir, the Jewish aggression against Muslims in Lebanon, the presence of U.S. troops in Saudi Arabia, U.S. support of Israel, and sanctions against Iraq." [40]

The runners near the finish line at the Boston Marathon on April 15, 2013 were victims of blowback from two nearby pressure cooker bombs that exploded, killing three people and injuring an estimated 264 others. [41] That tragic incidence of blowback, or retaliation (only days after a U.S. drone bombing killed 17 civilians in Afghanistan) was just one of a dozen or so incidents in the last several years of terrorist attacks against American targets. [42] The recent gruesome beheadings of American journalists on foreign soil by members of the terrorist group ISIS (Islamic State in Iraq and Syria) are gruesome examples of blowback that cannot be expected to end until America's gruesome war habit ends.

A few comments are pertinent here about the ISIS. It is a perfect example of how US foreign and military policy, motivated purely by self-interests is like a pin ball ricocheting here and there in a self-contained game machine. The ISIS was originally supported by the U.S. and its British ally as a means to counter other terrorist groups in the Greater Middle East so as to drive a wedge among the regimes in that part of the world and ultimately to dominate them and exploit their countries' resources. [43]

America will never be secure from retaliatory terror as long as she continues to terrorize. That is simply common sense and also is predictable by two laws and one principle. One law, the law of physics says for every action there is a reaction. The second law, the law of human nature says when a people can no longer tolerate inhumanities they will strike back. The principle is that of retributive justice, or "an eye for an eye." The possibility of continuous blowback on American soil or perhaps a "final blowback" or "a mass of bodies for a mass of bodies" is an ominous scenario of America's future. We will return to this scenario in the last chapter.

The national security that costs taxpayers so dearly and profits the spy business so clearly is false security. As long as America militarily intervenes and spies whenever and wherever she chooses she will never enjoy any sense of security and thus must constantly be on guard against blowback in one form or another.

Besides blowback being a roadblock to achieving real national security, the "intelligence" community is its own roadblock. "If we are so smart why are we so dumb?" asked Robert Scheer. He was referring to our national intelligence community made up of some 16 spy agencies (and maybe some too secret to be known) and countless (1,000 and more) spy contractors. Mr. Scheer went on to say, "'We know everything but learn nothing' would be an honest slogan for the NSA, CIA and lesser-known spy agencies that specialize in leading us so dangerously astray. For all of their massive intrusion into the personal lives of individuals throughout the world, it is difficult to

64

recall a time when the 'intelligence' they collected provided such myopic policy insight." [44]

This is the underworld of spooks that concocted the hair brained and botched "Bay of Pigs" invasion. Its bureaucratic bungling and in-fighting failed to prevent the "9/11" airstrikes, which could have been avoided altogether. [45]. Before tiring of the kindergarten exercise, the spooks bombarded Americans with daily color-coded threat warnings; the spooks have since discarded the colors for basic black. [46] The 2012 attack in Benghazi, Libya, was an intelligence fiasco. [47] The spooks "pissed" off the foreign leaders spied upon. [48] The spooks once had a hair brained scheme to allow anonymous gamblers to bet on the chance of assassinations and terrorists' attack and win money if the events occurred. [49] The spooks track on-line game playing and even create make-believe characters as spy aids; its CIA operatives childishly and chillingly refer to their drone strikes as "you track'em, we whack'em." [50] The spooks are suffocating under an avalanche of warrantless and incomprehensible data collected on millions of Americans. The spooks vastly underestimated the number of terrorists making up the relatively new but mushrooming threat of blowback from the Islamic State of Iraq and Syria [51]. And try as the spooks may to guard their secrets, someone like whistleblower Edward Snowden comes along and spills them. Does this make you wonder about the intelligence in the intelligence community?

The Monetary Costs

I have deliberately put discussion of the monetary costs last. Whatever they really are compared to the officially reported costs and however astronomical they are pale beside the costs already discussed. Money doesn't matter to the dead. Money won't matter if Armageddon comes. Yet, the monetary costs must be considered as a piece of the total accounting of the habits' burdens on America.

Calculating its total monetary costs since America's founding or even just for the last year would be more than an accountant's nightmare, it would be an impossible task, like counting sand on the beach. The meaning of "total monetary cost" is so broad and includes so many intangibles that it defies calculation. This cost involves three basic components, each itself very broad. The first would require an accounting of all conceivable inputs such as the costs of war contractors and military inputs such as the cost of troops. The second would require an accounting of all conceivable costs involving the process of conducting military interventions, such as those involving troop deployments. The third would require an accounting of the costs of all the consequences of the military intervention (assuming it came to an end) such as the expense of the medical treatment of survivors, of rebuilding damaged infrastructures, ad infinitum.

So the closest approximation to the total monetary cost necessarily is a distant approximation and one that is limited to the costs incurred by America and not also by the countries targeted. David Johnston, veteran reporter and tax and regulatory expert, has done a herculean job of attempting to estimate "the true cost of national security." He estimates that maintaining national security for the fiscal year 2013 cost over $1.3 trillion. In addition to accounting for the military budget, his estimate includes the national intelligence budget, the budget of the nuclear bomb-making arm of the Energy Department, the Homeland Security budget for customs and border patrol, the Coast Guard budget, the Veterans Affairs budget, and interest costs from debt-financing (tax revenues don't cover the entire costs). He notes that his total estimate "almost equals the $1.6 trillion expected to be raised through the individual federal income tax in fiscal 2013, [and thus] "doesn't leave much for other spending on commonwealth goods and services that provide the foundation for private incomes and wealth." [52]

An Aside: The Drug War

Note that Mr. Johnston's estimate does not include the "war on drugs" carried out by the Drug Enforcement Agency (DEA) and its contractors. Their surveillance, sniffing, and interdictions cost America over 2.05 billion in 2013. [53] Perhaps Mr. Johnston does not think the "war on drugs" meets the definition of "war." Perhaps not, but the DEA uses the paraphernalia of war; "airplanes, ships, helicopter, and radar." [54]

Note that Mr. Johnston's estimate does include the national intelligence budget ("just" $52.6 billion for FY 2013) to pay for America's quasi police state with its 16 spy agencies and their some 1,000 contractors that monitor and intimidate her citizens.

Overall Economic Costs

As with household budgets, the national budget accrues two kinds of debt, good and bad. Good debt stems from borrowing money to pay for socially constructive investments in say education with positive returns such as a more educated public. Bad debt is money owed for bad national habits that have negative returns, such as the aforementioned "sadtistical" condition of America. Bad national debts produce a sick country and a sickly economy. Bad debt from Cold War expenses, not Ronald

Reagan, collapsed the Soviet Union. If bad national debt continues to accumulate, it will eventually bankrupt America. Adam Smith, the 18th century founder of capitalism clearly understood the drag of military costs on an economy, and argued that military spending was economically unproductive. The counter argument that millions of jobs tied to warring and spying would be lost is easily refuted. Slashing the war/spy budget in half would free up the other half for the economy to use in creating productive jobs to more than replace the lost jobs. [55]

Endnotes

1. Wilson, S.B. Op. cit.
2. Wilson, S.B. Op. cit.
3. Lucas, JA. Deaths In Other Nations Since WW II Due To Us Interventions. Countercurrents.org, April 24, 2007.
4. Eckhardt, W. "Civilian deaths in wartime." Security Dialogue, 2008 (1), 89-98. See also, Roberts, PC. July 4th Militarist Bunkum (an encore by request). Roberts/paulcraigroberts.org/ July 3, 2014.
5. Lamb, F. US Officials Confess to Targeting Iran's Civilian Population. Cyrano's Journal, February 16 2013.
6. 60 Minutes, May 12, 1996.
7. Hedges, C. Murder Is Not an Anomaly in War. Truth Dig, March 19, 2012.
8. Moore, M. Will They Ever Trust Us Again? Letters from the War Zone. Simon & Schuster, 2004.
9. Madrak, S. Soldier's Mom: Military Suicides Are 'Out of Control.' Crooks & Liars, November 27, 2012.
10. Pollitt, K. America Doesn't Torture'—It Kills. The Nation, February 13, 2013.
11. Huffington, A. 'Signature Strikes' and the President's Empty Rhetoric on Drones.
Huff Post Politics, July 10, 2013.

12. Engelhardt, T. The US Has Bombed at Least Eight Wedding Parties Since 2001. The Nation, December 20, 2013.

13. Englehardt, Op Cit.

14. Benjamin, M. Drones Have Come Out Of the Shadows. Dissident Voice, November 4, 2013.

15. Benjamin, Op. Cit.

16. Chossudovsky, M. The Children Killed by America's Drones. "Crimes Against Humanity" committed by Barack H. Obama. Global Research Center for Research on Globalization, January 26, 2013.

17. Kimbereley, M. Freedom Rider: Killing Children. Cyrano's Journal, January 5, 2013.

18. Scheer, R. America's Global Torture Network. OpEdNews, February 8, 2013.

19. Van Buren, P. Torture Superpower. TomDispatch.com, December 18, 2012.

20. Van Buren, P. Ibid.

21. Project Censored. US Department of Defense is the Worst Polluter on the Planet. /www.projectcensored.org/2-us-department-of-defense-is-the-worst-polluter-on-the-planet; Sanders, B. The Green Zone: The Environmental Costs of Militarism. AK Press, 2009; and Veterans for Peace. The True Costs of War: www.veteransforpeace.org/our-work/true-costs-war/true-cost-of-war-to-our-environment.

22. Scheer, R. No Place to Hide: We're All Suspects in Barack Obama's America. OpEdNews, January 21, 2014.

23. Riechmann, D. NSA Spying Controversy Angers Foreign Leaders, Threatens U.S. Foreign Policy. Associated.Press and Lubbock Avalanche Journal, October26,2013.

24. Nader, R. The Ralph Nader Reader. Seven Stories Press, 2000.

25. Brumback, GB. The Meaning of Freedom and the Half Mad Hatters of the Tea Party. Dissident Voice, September 23, 2010.

26. Thiele, E. Military Spending: Cost of Iraq War is but the Tip of the Iceberg. Global Research Online, June 14, 2010, www.globalresearch.ca.

27. Brumback, GB. The Devil's Marriage: Break Up the Corpocracy or Leave Democracy in the Lurch. Author House; 2011. Chapter 9, 141.

28. Some sources on America's dismal condition: Blow, CM. Empire at the End of Decadence. New York Times, February 18, 2011; Buchheit, P. Five Facts That Put America to Shame. Common Dreams, May 14, 2012; Froomkin, D. Occupy Right Again: U.S. Near Bottom In New Social Justice Index. HuffPostBusiness, October 27, 2011; Sullivan, T. An America In Retreat? Crooks & Liars, July 15, 2013; and Zuesse, E. How the U.S. Performs in Recent International Rankings; Hint: 3rd, as in Third World. OpEdNews, April 15, 2013.

29. See War Resisters League. How Could Our Tax Money Be Used? www.warresisters.org/militaryspending

30. Josephson, M. Teaching ethical decision-making and principled reasoning. Ethics: Easier Said than Done, Issue #1, 1988, 27-33.

31. Ross, S. More Than 30 Top U.S. Officials Guilty of War Crimes, Boyle Says. OpEdNews.com, December 11, 2012.

32. Brumback, GB. Is America Going to Hell in a Handbasket? The Greanville Post, March 29, 2013; Uncommon Thought Journal, April 21, 2013; and Cyrano's Journal, April 22, 2013.

33. Boyle, FA. American Militarism Threatening To Set Off World War III. OpEdNews, December 12, 2012; Lendman, S. Another Century of War. OpEdNews, December 12, 2011; and Roberts, PC. Pushing Toward The Final War. OpEdNews, March 28, 2014.

34. quotationsbook.com.

35. Swanson, D. War Is A Lie. OpEdNews, March 7, 2013.

36. Caplan, L. Leaks and Consequences: Why Treating Leakers as Spies Puts Journalists at Legal Risk. The American Scholar, Autumn Issue, 2013, 20-31.

37. Rich, F. Will the Real Traitors Please Stand Up? The New York Times Online, May 14, 2006.

38. Roberts, PC. The Five Criminals: In America the Gestapo Has Replaced The Rule Of Law. OpEdNews, February 13, 2014.

39. Gladwell, M. Trust No One. The New Yorker, July 28, 2014, 70-75. The book Mr. Gladwell reviewed was A Spy Among Friends: Kim Philby and the Great Betrayal by Ben Macintyre, Crown, 2014

40. Wikipedia. Motives for the September 11 Attacks.

41. Helman, SR. & Russell, J. The Long Mile Home. Dutton, 2014.

42. Blum, W. Blindness to Blowback. OpEdNews. May 4, 2013.

43. Ahmed, N. How The West Created ISIS. Popular Resistance Daily Digest, September 18, 2014.

44. Scheer, R. NSA, Benghazi and the Monsters of Our Own Creation. OpEdNews, December 31, 2013.

45. There is no better short summary of the inexcusable, bordering on criminal way in which the national intelligence community mishandled intelligence about events and terrorists before 9/11 than the one and one-half page piece in the New Yorker by its staff writer, Lawrence Wright: The Al Qaeda Switchboard. January 13, 2014, 17-18.

46. Ryan, J. Terror Alert Color Code Fades to Black: New Threat Warning System Coming Online. ABC News, April 20, 2011.

47. Scheer, R. Op.Cite. 2013.

48. Lindorff, D. Is America playing its last card? Pissing Off Friends is a Doomed Strategy. OpEdNews. August 6, 2013.

49. Lizza, R. State of Deception. The New Yorker, December 16, 2013, 48-61, 53.

50. Ibid., 55. See also, Elliott, J. & Mazzetti, M. World of Spycraft: NSA and CIA Spied in Online Games. The New YorkTimes,December9,2013.

51. Portno, H. According to New CIA Report, White House Underestimated ISIS's Strength. www.examiner.com , September 13, 2014.

52. Johnston, DC. The True Cost of National Security. Columbia Journalism Review, January 31, 2013.

53. DEA. http://www.justice.gov/jmd/2013summary. Press and Lubbock Avalanche Journal, October 26, 2013.

54. Schwartz, M. A Mission Gone Wrong: Why are We Still Fighting the Drug War? The New Yorker, January 6, 2014, 44-55.

55. Dumas, L. Economic Conversion. Public Sphere Project, University of Texas at Dallas, undated. http://www.publicsphereproject.org/node/240. For other sources on the effect on job creation of military spending see the following e.g.,: Brown, EH. The Military as a Jobs Program: There are More Efficient Ways to Stimulate an Economy. Dissident Voice, June 23, 2011; and Froomkin, D. Military Spending Costs Jobs, Doesn't Create Them, Anti-War Group Says. HuffPostPolitics, September 13, 2011.

CHAPTER 3
BLACK BOXES AND BADVANTAGES

Calling them habits does not explain them. What does is a "human equation" that explains all human behavior, including repetitive behavior, which is precisely what a habit is. [1] It may just be the most important non mathematical equation you will ever see in your life. As a matter of fact it explains your life. Here is what the equation looks like:

$$\text{The Person} + \text{The Situation}$$
$$=$$
$$\text{The Person's Behavior} + \text{The Consequences}$$

This is a universal equation. It is the same for every human being on earth, whether butcher, baker, candle stick maker, U.S. president, CEO, drone operator, mole, the homeless; in other words, everyone.

The explanation for all human behavior is on the left side of the equation, where you see two inputs. Behavior never happens without both and will never be fully explained without both. Without a person there would be no behavior, no habit. Without the circumstances and conditions of situations there also would be no behavior, no habit, because no one lives totally isolated from one's surroundings. Thus, human behavior is determined by human beings' circumstance as well as by human beings themselves.

Of course, every person has his or her own particular equation, sort of like the person's unique DNA code. The particulars can change from day to day for a given individual, except some of the particulars for chronic habits change less.

"Black box" is a metaphor that stands for the person in the equation. I did not coin the metaphor. Its origin came from calling some psychologists years ago "black box psychologists" because they believed situations totally explained human behavior and whatever the characteristics of the person were didn't matter and thus could be left unknown as if they were in a black box. You can tell from my equation that I am not a black box psychologist.

I did coin the term "badvantage." It stands for situations that tempt or pressure the person to behave badly in order to satisfy the temptation or relieve the pressure. Any badvantage, therefore, gives an advantage to bad behavior.

So in order to explain America's warring and spying habits, which are the sine qua non of bad behavior, one has to know what the black boxes and badvantages are of the people most responsible for that behavior, starting with the person in the Oval Office.

I am going to speculate on what the black boxes and badvantages are for President Barack Obama and his immediate predecessor, George Bush. I am not picking on these two presidents. I could have picked other former occupants of the Oval Office. Their black boxes and badvantages would have generally been the same.

The Black Boxes of Bush and Obama

Their DNA

Some research suggests that a particular gene is more likely to be found among leaders than followers. [2] Other research suggests that a person's genetic makeup may to some extent predispose the person to a life of crime. [3] "Putting two and two together," is it much of a stretch to wonder if their genes have at least a minor influence on their committing international war crimes?

TheirGender

Do you know of any female U.S. president? Wars throughout history have been started and fought by males with very few exceptions (Cleopatra and Margaret Thatcher, for example). While testosterone may play a tiny role in a male leader's aggression, we live in a male dominated society, which means among other things that males are expected to dominate and to be aggressive when confronted with conflicts.

Their Background

A person's background is the person's history, and you know the old saying, "history is prologue to the future." There's a grain or more of truth to it, and more so when some of the person's behavior is habitual since a habit is the past repeated, is it not? A person's background tells us how that person's characteristics have evolved and what role they played in the person's lifetime of responses to a lifetime of situations.

Bush was born with a silver spoon in his mouth so to speak and a member of a dynasty with a sense of entitlement that sometimes surfaced on the wrong side of the law and with impunity. [4] His father, George Walker Bush, before becoming the first U.S. president in the Bush family had been a director of the CIA.

Obama's parents were allegedly on the CIA payroll and that agency reportedly "financed his college education and gave him his first job afterwards." [5] Is he indebted to the CIA? Is he afraid of the CIA given its history of assassinations? I will return to the matter of the influence the "shadow government" (i.e., CIA and NSA) allegedly has on whoever sits in the Oval Office when we get to the other part of the human equation.

Their Personalities

Let's turn now to their personalities and raise some questions about whether these socially undesirable personality traits; greed/ambition, morally unprincipled, narcissism and close mindedness are associated with their kind of leadership behavior.

Greedy/Ambitious?

We know they are ambitious. Anyone is who climbs up to the Oval Office.

Morally Unprincipled?

Anyone who starts a war against another nation on a pretext or who orders drone strikes is morally unprincipled and will do whatever is necessary to achieve desired ends. Bush, a born-again Christian would naturally disagree. So would Obama. Let's hear what the latter himself has said about his own moral character: "---I think I'm pretty good at keeping my moral compass while recognizing that I am a product of original sin." [6] The subordinating clause of that statement is a perfect example of a moral rationalization as in, "well, we all sin in our own ways." And again in his own words: "One of the things that I've learned to appreciate more as President is you are essentially a relay swimmer in a river full of rapids, and that river is history." [7] In other words, you can blame what he's doing on history. And he's partly right.

To the extent that any war/spy commander in chief has any hint of morality it is compartmentalized, a form of moral rationalization and a habit typical of most humans. Certain mental compartments are reserved for scruples and others for behavior ranging from the less scrupulous to evil. I will give you one example from Obama's repertoire of behavior. A few days after he had eulogized Dr. Martin Luther King, the antiwar activist when alive, the president announced he would be doing some more bombing. [8]

Now, we can interpret that seeming contradiction in two ways. Either his eulogy was nothing other than posturing, which is second nature to politicians, or he was pulling the eulogy out of a moral compartment and deciding from a different compartment to go bombing again. Either way, he was at worst exhibiting unprincipled morality and at best conditional morality.

Narcissistic?

What national leader isn't narcissistic? An extreme form of narcissism is a sense of grandiosity, as President Obama seems to display in this remark; "Here's my bottom line, America must always lead on the stage. If we don't, no one else will." [9] Another extreme form is a lack of empathy. Have you ever seen the two of them express empathy or remorse over innocent people killed by their military decisions? Sometime after I wrote that last sentence I spotted an article in the New Yorker quoting Obama in a speech to the National Defense University saying about civilian deaths from drones that such incidents are "heartbreaking tragedies" that would be haunting memories for "as long as we live." [10] I think his expressed remorse was mostly posturing rather than being deeply felt especially since he went on to defend the use of drones.

Hubris is another element of this personality trait. It was displayed by President Bush standing on the deck of an aircraft carrier and boasting "mission accomplished;" and in this boastful remark; "The interesting thing about being president is that you don't feel like [you] owe anybody an explanation.[11]

Psychopathic?

It would not be unusual if Bush and Obama were psychopathic. Apparently it is "normal" if we can believe the findings from a study that relied on some 100 historical experts' analyses of data on all U.S. presidents. The researchers say they found this personality trait in every U.S. president. [12] Noted psychoanalyst Dr. Justin Frank seems to have found it also when analyzing the backgrounds and behavior of Bush and Obama. [13]

Close-minded?

Ron Suskind was the senior national-affairs reporter for The Wall Street Journal from 1993 to 2000 and the author of a book and articles about Bush. Mr. Suskind writes that when asked by his top deputies to explain his decisions "the president would say that he relied on his 'gut' or his 'instinct' to guide the ship of state, and then he 'prayed over it.'" [14] Anyone believing their decisions is guided by the supernatural are not likely to open their mind to alternative decisions.

As for President Obama, he once told a reporter; "And every morning and every night I'm taking measure of my actions against the options and possibilities available to me---." [15] Now that statement suggests he's open-minded, but he certainly has been close minded about ending the drone strikes and reaching out to the world with an olive branch.

Close-mindedness is the personality trait that seems to be the most correlated with less intelligence. The more close-minded a person is, the more to suspect that person is not as intelligent as an open-minded person. That may be why the policy decisions and actions of Bush and Obama have seemed so mindless. Habits, after all, don't require any superior intelligence or critical thinking.

Beliefs?

Firmly held beliefs are like ideologies that have hardened into certainties. Nowhere is that more pronounced than in the case of religious beliefs, where believing becomes seeing, not the other way around. More down to earth, a pronounced belief of every American president is that of manifest destiny, the belief, no, the certainty that America is destined to be the leader of the world. The neoconservatives and neoliberals of today that bend the ears of our presidents are living examples of this ideology in action. The invasion of Iraq, for example, was planned long before 9/11 by influential neoconservatives with connections to the White House. [16] Another pronounced belief, so intuitive and counter intuitive at the same time, is the conviction, or maybe a rationalization if the belief is a pretense, that certain wars, America's wars most certainly, are always "just and necessary." We shall collide with that conviction in Appendix A.

Selfish Purpose?

Absolutely. As with Bush and all previous U.S. presidents, Obama is acting for his own self-interests, not for the interests of the American people, even though he will most certainly disagree and would, I'm sure, argue he is acting in the best interests of America. If that is true, his actions have certainly failed in any case.

Purpose, along with intentions and expectations, are an extremely strong influencer on human behavior. They help motivate and guide it.

Ordinary, simple habits don't need an explicit purpose. Take the case of the cigarette smoker ((but don't take him/her in the same room). That habit basically drives itself. The need for and sight of a cigarette is all that is needed to keep the habit alive. The warring and spying habits, by virtue of their enormity of scale, need self and publicly proclaimed purposes.

Why Do Americans Elect Such Black Boxes?

The answer, I think, is two-fold. First, American voters have little say in the selection and election of their presidents. The Constitution's specification of the dysfunctional Electoral College, the government's controlled Federal Election Commission, and corporate campaign financing guarantee that the "twin" parties' candidates will dominate the ballots. Second, we shall see in Chapter 6 how American education is one of an addicted regime's most reliable "habit helpers." It is never

80

in any regime's advantage to have most if not all citizens educated to think for themselves. If they did there would be an entirely different and better America. Psychologist David Dunning and sociologist Mato Nagel have theorized and showed through a computer simulated election that incompetent people can't judge leadership qualities. [17] That finding is not accidental. America's regimes' plan it thatway.

Their Badvantages

Any president of America probably has more badvantages than any other living human being. As I see it, there are at leasteightofthem.

Seductive Positions

History is replete with leaders seduced by the powerful positions they held. Power is readily available to be exploited and abused. The U.S. presidency is certainly a seductive position, but its power, as with all seductive positions, is usually moderated to some extent by the relative strength s and weaknesses of the other badvantages and any countervailing or oppositional forces.

Organizational Size

The bigger an organization is the more unmatched is the power available to the organization's leaders to wield and usually with impunity. Needless to say to America's taxpayers and to the rest of the world, the U.S. government is the biggest national government in the world.

Hierarchical Organizational Structure

Large organizations like governments and corporations are hierarchies with "pecking orders." People at and near the top do the ordering and people below follow them. The hierarchy is a perfect place to order wrongdoing to be done and then to blame it on people at the lower levels.

Organizational and Social Culture

Culture, whether that of a government agency, a corporation, or that of a society is like an autobiography that says, "This is our history, who we are, what we believe, what we value, and how we operate." Any U.S. president, like most people whether plebeians or potentates, operates within both an organizational and social culture and is influenced by it to varying degrees in varying situations.

As an illustration let's consider briefly and first President Obama's organizational culture and zero in on its most potent element, namely, his "shadow government" made up primarily of the CIA, the NSA, and the military. His shadow government influences, if not sometimes predetermines his decisions if we can believe the authenticity of reports from various sources, a few of which I will cite here.

The reason why Obama blocked criminal persecutions of officials in the previous administration according to various sources is that he was worried that "the CIA, NSA and military would revolt" and he reminded his confidants of "what had happened to Martin Luther King," an implicit allusion to the alleged assassination arranged by the CIA. [18] If Obama did not also mention the assassination of President Kennedy under similar circumstances it was probably too discomforting for him to have done so.

From a few other sources have come reports that also seem to cast doubt on Obama's unilateral authority. We learn, for instance, that   he told the vice-chairman of the Joint Chiefs of Staff who was whining to him about the CIA's getting a disproportionate share of the war pie that "The CIA gets what it wants." [19] And we hear indirectly from Senator Ron Wyden, member of the Senate Select Committee on Intelligence and who reportedly has had "'several spirited discussions' with Obama," that "It really seems like General Clapper, the intelligence leadership, and the lawyers drive this in terms of how decisions get made at the White House." [20]

Not being privy to either Obama's mind or to his inner circle, what are we to make of such reports? Are Obama, and were his predecessors, puppets or puppeteers? What I make of it is simply that President Obama, just like the rest of us, does not live in a vacuum. He is not the sole reason why he does what he does. His human equation has that other input.

Another part of Obama's organizational culture of course is the political one in the form of the U.S. Congress. It is dominated by the party twins, Democrats and Republicans. Any U.S. president can count on any Congress being almost to a person war and spy hawks. If there were any doubts about these hawks and their dependence on the war and spy industries Chapters 4 and 5 ought to dispel them.

Now let's turn for a moment to Obama's much larger context, the culture of the society in which he lives. It is perfectly suited for his position and its shadowy government for it is a sociopathic culture that not only accepts but expects endless warring and spying. [21] This second culture is a creature of the first but they feed off each other.

Upside- Down Incentives

U.S. presidents and corporate CEOs are addicted to them. An upside down incentive, as you can probably guess, is one that rewards bad behavior and/or punishes good behavior. The most egregious upside down incentive is the case of U.S. warriors-in-chief and their regimes never having to worry about being prosecuted as war criminals by the International Criminal Court to which the U.S. deliberately did not join. International war criminals these people are, stupid they are not. Another potent upside down incentive is provided by the U.S. Supreme Court's ruling that corporations (including those in the war and spy industries) are persons and thus allowed to finance the campaigns of politicians, rendering them mouthpieces for their corporate patrons (see Chapter 4).

Incentives, upside down and right side up, are the crux of black box psychology, where no brain is needed, except for that of these psychologists (if there are any left). To them, an incentive is the carrot or stick of all human behavior. Use the first to encourage behavior and the second to discourage behavior. If only a massive and insurmountable mix of right side up carrots and sticks could be brewed to stop warriors and spies in their tracks.

Best or Worst of Times

The best of times, which stokes greed, tends to bring out the worst in human nature just as the worst of times, which stokes need, tends to do the same. Fortune 500 companies, for instance, tend to get into legal trouble more often when

84

times are good. In the case of U.S. presidents, however, the worst of times is when they get more militaristic. The difference is that an American regime in its militaristic imperialism creates its own worst of times by turning potential friends into enemies. Nothing boosts its profits and power and distracts the home folks from domestic plight more than having an enemy or two or three. Making sure America has enemies is a very potent badvantage for a U.S. president. Think about it for a moment. The U.S. is thousands of miles across water and land from her enemies that wouldn't be America's enemies if America stayed at home. But when has her imperialistic regimes ever stayed at home?

Global Enticements

Globalization is the contemporary euphemism for imperialism or "global gobbling." The globe is one giant opportunity for market expansion, resource exploitation and political manipulation by the more powerful nations, which helps explain why U.S. regimes try to be the most powerful of all. The prospect of installing or protecting dictatorships to protect U.S. corporate investments on foreign soil in the pretext of spreading and defending freedom is just too much of a temptation for CEOs and U.S. presidents alike to resist.

One of the most alluring global plumbs up for gobbling has always been oil. The engines of America's corpocracy run on oil. That dependency goes a long way toward explaining American imperialism.

The Powerful Corpocracy and Its Allies

America's corpocracy, the "Devil's Marriage" between big government and big business, along with the duo's allies (see Chapter 6) are a gigantic, endless badvantage for all people in and associated with the corpocracy and its corporate driven political and economic systems, not just with the corpocracy's warring and spying component. [22] They all feed off one another at the expense of the public. Large corporations, including those in the defense and intelligence industries expect and get countless favors and the subservient government's politicians provide them in exchange for public office. It is truly a Devil's Marriage.

There you have it, eight badvantages, and there's absolutely no doubt that every one of them has tempted or pressured not only President Obama but also his predecessors. The badvantages help explain and influence but do not exonerate their negative leadership (i.e., bad behavior and bad results for the common people). Leaders, like everyone else, are responsible and must be held accountable for their own behavior and its consequences; that they never are held accountable can be blamed on the badvantages.

The Habits' Roots

The black boxes and badvantages we have just reviewed are the two habits' roots so to speak. I am reluctant to name a "mother root" such as corporate driven capitalism for example because all of the roots are tightly intertwined. Thus, while the reforms proposed in Chapter 7 concentrate on the war and spy component of the corpocracy they ought to have some spillover effect on the rest of the corpocracy, particularly when it comes to reforms of a political nature.

On Being Human and Humane

The human equation helps to understand and predict behavior but says nothing about what it means to be human. To be human means to me being borne one as trite as that is true for me to say. But there is nothing trite and everything both simple and profound in Professor John McDonnell Tierney's little book, On Being Human. To him it means being "a caring, compassionate, and kind sentient entity-stewards of the Earth." I would call that being a humane human and it is a tough bar to reach. He says that we are not there yet; that we are a "work in progress." [23] I would like to think that some of us are nearly there; and I would think everyone instrumental in warring and spying, including the two characters featured in this chapter are works in regress who will remain inhumane without being held accountable, without personal atonement, and without ending their inhumane behavior.

On Learning to Kill

U.S. presidents order the killing. They do not do the actual killing. We have to go down to the bottom of the echelon of warring and spying to find the underlings who activate the deadly weapons aimed at other human beings. That takes us, for example, inside boot camp where these underlings are taught and then ordered to kill because it is unnatural for human beings to kill other human beings on a massive scale. Were it natural our species would either be extinct by now or substantially depleted. Were it natural there would be no skyrocketing cases of post traumatic syndrome or suicides among soldiers.

Here is what a former Army ranger had to say about the crucial role of military training in learning to kill: "Military training is fundamentally an exercise in overcoming a fear of killing another human." [24] This enterprising ranger has gone on to form a consulting group, "Killology Research Group," a bunch of "Warrior Science Group consultants dedicated to protecting our families and our children and to the strong defense of our country." [25] Nothing surprises me anymore after reading the ranger's website.

Think about it. Our government takes our youth, often under privileged, and turns them into killers so that politicians can stay in office and the business driver of the corpocracy can keep on thriving, not dying.

Endnotes

1. I first conceived of the idea of the human equation in my book on organizational performance: Tall Performance from Short Organizations through We/Me Power. 1st Books Library, 2002.
2. Prigg, M. The Secret to being a Great Leader? It's in your Genes, Researchers Say. Daily Mall, January 15, 2013.
3. Cohen, P. Genetic Basis for Crime: A New Look. The New York Times, June 19, 2011.4. 4. Parry, R. Secrecy & Privilege: The Rise of the Bush Dynasty from Watergate to Iraq. The Media Consortium, 2004.
5. Ross, S. Obama's Ties to CIA May Explain His Totalitarian Views. Veterans Today, May 3, 2013.
6. Remnick, D, Going the Distance: On and Off the Road with Barack Obama. The New Yorker, January 27, 2014, 41-61, 61.
7. Ibid., 61.
8. Sirota, D. What Happened to the Anti-War Movement? Nation of Change, September 6, 2013.

9. Blum, W. What Would a Psychiatrist Call This? Delusions of Grandeur? The Anti-Empire Report #130. Dissident Voice, July 12, 2014.

10. Coll, S. The Unblinkable Stare. The New Yorker, November 24, 2014, 98-109.

11. Nader, R. A Letter to George Bush. Dissident Voice, January 1, 2014.

12. Howard, J. Psychopathic Personality Traits Linked With U.S. Presidential Success, Psychologists Suggest. The Huffington Post, September 13, 2012.

13. Frank, J. Bush on the Couch. Harper Perennial, 2005. Obama on the Couch. Free Press, 2012.

14. Suskind, R. Faith, Certainty and the Presidency of George W. Bush. The New York Times Magazine, October 17, 2004; and, Suskind, R. The Price of Loyalty: George W. Bush, the White House, and the Education of Paul O'Neill. Simon & Schuster, 2004.

15. Remnick. Op. Cit., 61.

16. There are many accounts of how 9/11 was a golden opportunity for Bush and gang, including his neoconservative tutors to carry out a plan years in the making to invade Iraq. See, e.g., Battle, J. The Iraq War-Part I: The U.S. Prepares for Conflict, The National Security Archive, 2001; Beversdorf, T. The Most Essential Lesson of History That No One Wants to Admit. First Rebuttal, December 7, 2014; and Weber, M. Iraq: A War For Israel. Institute for Historical Review, March, 2008.

17. Wolchover, N. People Aren't Smart Enough for Democracy to Flourish, Scientists Say. OpEdNews, February 28, 2012.

18. Swanson, D. Mark Udall and the Unspeakable. Dissident Voice, November 22, 2014.

19. Coll, S. Remote Control: Our Drone Delusion. The New Yorker, May 6, 2003, 77.

20. Lizza, R. State of Deception: Why Won't the President Rein in the Intelligence Community? The New Yorker, December 16, 2013, 48-61, 50.

21. Derber, C. Sociopathic Society: A People's Sociology of the United States. Paradigm Publishers, 2013. See also, Lewis, AR. The American Culture of War: A History of US Military Force from World War II to Operation Enduring Freedom. Routledge, 2012.

22. Brumback, G.B. The Devil's Marriage: The Devil's Marriage: Break Up the Corpocracy or Leave Democracy in the Lurch, Bloomington, IN: Author House, 2011.

23. Tierney, JM. On Being Human, Dreamsinger Little Books, 2011.

24. Carey, B. Psychologists Explain Iraq Airstrike Video. New York Times, April 7, 2011.The Army ranger quoted in this article is Lt. Col. Dave Grossman, author of the book "On Killing: The Psychological Cost of Learning to Kill in War and Society. Back Bay Books, 2009.

25. Killology Research Group. A Warrior Science Group Partner. http://killology.com.

CHAPTER 4
THE ADDICTED GOVERNMENT

As I've said, government America and corporate America are in the Devil's bed together. Corporate America is in the driver's seat, or "missionary position," take your pick. When it comes to the warring and spying part of the corpocracy, however, it may be a tossup as to who is on top. But it doesn't really matter in this case. Both government and industry seem to outdo themselves in being a badvantage for each other. If either one or both were to be totally reformed for the sake of peace and freedom America's two habits would be broken.

In America's Constitution government is divided among three branches to prevent government from being a monolithic monster. It has never worked that way. Instead of checking and balancing each other's manner and boundaries of governing, the three branches march in lock step to the beat of corporate America, even though corporations are not mentioned in America's original blueprint.

What we are dealing with here is a three-headed government monster. The three heads obviously work a bit differently from each other but all have the same addictions and all work with a common purpose, to ensure that America dominates the world. They all belong to what I call officialdom's "Land of the Habbits," with apologies to J.R. R. Tolkien. Let's take a look at this three-headed monster one head at a time. [1]

The Executive Addiction
Grave Choices by the Supreme War Commander

The U.S. president is the supreme commander- in-chief. In America's history that totals 42 warriors-in-chiefs and spies-in-chief. So far there have been 44 presidents but remember that two died before they could do any warring and spying.

Who knows how many people our 42 presidents have sent to their graves? Counting declared wars and other overt and covert military interventions gives me an overall impression.. It will have to do, and it's really all I need to do since one death by force is one too many Based on the results of my research reported in Chapter 2 I would hazard a guess of 25 to 30 million graves having been dug with more being dug before this sentence is ended.

President Obama has the distinction of being the first warrior-in-chief to sit down with his aides, pour over a potential "hit list" of supposed terrorists, and then select those "suspects" as targets for drone strikes. If there is a Devil, I doubt if that underworld character could have devised a more devilish scheme.

President Obama trotted out his "chief counterterrorism advisor" (before the latter became the new CIA director) to promote his death by drone policy. One of the occasions for doing so was a speech his advisor gave at the Woodrow Wilson International Center. In his speech the chief claimed drone strikes were "efficacious," "ethical" and "legal." [2] In response I wrote and got published an "unsent letter" to the chief in which I rebutted each of his three claims. [3] The drone strikes continued even if I had sent it.

I voted for Mr. Obama because the alternative choices in a rigged election system were far more preferable but unrealistic. I will be telling you in Chapter 7 about a letter I sent him with a proposed inaugural address after his first victory. The gist of the proposal was a commitment to world peace and how to achieve it. Like my open letter, it was ignored.

The Executive Addiction
Spying by the Supreme Spy Commander

Presumably supreme spy commanders don't do the actual spying any more than the one and same supreme war commanders do the actual warring. I suspect given its shadowy nature there is more renegade spying than renegade warring. Did President Kennedy, for example, know or care about his FBI director monitoring the president's philandering?

I have no idea which president has been the supreme of the supreme spy chiefs, but I would guess that ever since WWII they have been actively involved in ordering significant spying operations and numerous reorganizations of the intelligence arm of the executive bureaucracy.

From the foregoing look at the executive branch, should we conclude that it is the most evil and lawless of the three? That was the rhetorical question raised not long ago by Fred Branfman whose writings appear in the New York Times, the Washington Post, Harper's, many other publications, and who is the author of Voices from the Plain of Jars. "We almost never," he writes, "ask such questions in this country; never try to put ourselves in the shoes of the tens of millions of victims of our leaders' war-making because doing so confronts us with a grave dilemma. On the one hand, if we would say these acts are evil if done to ourselves they are obviously also evil when done to others. But admitting that would require most of us to challenge our most basic beliefs about this nation and its leadership. And if we are members of our political, intellectual, media, government and private sector elites, it would threaten our jobs and livelihoods." [4]

The Executive Addiction
The War and Spy Agencies

George Washington fought the American Revolution without any of them. Today, President Obama delegates that "work" to the subordinate chiefs of too many offices and agencies to count. They are listed in Appendix C. It may not be a complete list. Some offices and/or agencies may be hidden from public view, part of an invisible government so to speak.

Although the war and spy agencies are listed separately they overlap in their work. Notice on the list for instance that the military intelligence components dominate the spy bureaucracy. Author and journal editor Clay Risen noted in 2009 that "Military snooping on civilians, which escalated in the turbulent 60's, never entirely went away and is back again."[5] Well, Mr. Risen, when you thought it was partly gone I'd say it probably had partly gone underground for a while before resurfacing.

Knowing how organizations really are versus how they should be organized and run is one of my specialties. [6] But it doesn't take any specialty to see the obvious. Appendix C depicts an organizational structure of the worst kind, the classic hierarchical and bloated bureaucracy, which is not atypical of government or corporations.

The Department of Defense (DoD) and the Department of Homeland Security (DHS) are show cases for bureaucracy. DHS, a hodgepodge collection of 23 formerly separate agencies with a budget of around $40 billion and 240,00 employees is a testimony to how fast government, once it seizes on an opportunity, in this case the 9/11 catastrophe, can build a monumental house of cards. In no time flat it has become the third largest federal bureaucracy, one regarded as "being without direction" and ineffective to say the least. [7] The way it mishandled its response to Hurricane Katrina's devastation of parts of New Orleans is perhaps to date the agency's most well-known piece of ineptitude.

Represented in Appendix C are several million paid people. If all of them were moved to a new city out in the desert it would instantly become the fourth largest city in the U.S., which would make it easier for the rest of America to gather up enough nerve to close it down.

The agencies' work of interest that I want to sketch here involves their bookkeeping, buying war and spy supplies (e.g., deadly weaponry) from contractors, and their caring (mostly poorly) for veterans.

Bookkeeping

America's war and spy annual budget is not only second to none in the world, it is eight to none. That is, the U.S. budget is larger than the next eight countries' combined budgets. [8] With an annual budget of over one-half trillion dollars, a natural question to ask is how on earth does the DoD keep track of its incoming and outgoing money? There must be millions of dollars falling through the cracks every day.

Medea Benjamin, co-founder of the activist organization, Code Pink, tells us in one of her articles that former Secretary of Defense, Robert M. Gates once complained that "it was nearly impossible to get accurate information and answers to basic questions, such as "How much money did you spend?" and "How many people do you have?" [9] I personally think it was a hollow complaint. He knew very well that DoD can ignore with impunity the legal requirement to audit itself. Who's going to hold DoD accountable? Certainly not the warrior/spy-in-chief or any other federal agency and certainly not Congress or the Supreme Court.

Buying from Contractors

Uncle Sam is the Sugar Daddy for the thousands of weapons makers and all other makers and vendors in the warring and spying business. Stories about Sugar Daddy's profligacy, waste and inefficiency are legendary. A chief DoD buyer, officially known as the "Under Secretary of Defense for Acquisition, Technology and Logistics," once lamented that "We tend to retry things every 10 years or so because we don't remember what happened the last time they were tried. That is because we don't have any data. It takes data and in-depth analysis to understand what really works." [10]

In other words, DoD doesn't seem to know, or perhaps even to care, about what works and doesn't work in its bottomless inventory of weapons and all of its other overflowing material goods (read "material bads" as we shall see examples of in the next chapter).

The Forgotten Soldiers

One of my heart-felt convictions is reflected in this personal homily: "Mourn wars' victims, scorn the war lords." Inexcusably, among the millions of victims are America's forgotten soldiers and castoffs, paid lip service at ceremonies but essentially left to tend for themselves despite the mission and partly because of the bureaucracy of the Department of Veterans Affairs and the shameful Congress that penny pinches just that one piece of the gargantuan military budget.

Remember the heart breaking story of Army vet William Busbeer? His story is one of legions. A veteran commits suicide every 80 minutes. For every service member who dies in battle, 25 return and die by their own hands. [11]

A veteran's suicide is the latest stage of the clinically and abstractly sounding "post traumatic syndrome."[12] The earlier stages sound like stories of living Hell. In one of those stories a 25 year old soldier initially "thought of himself as a patriot---Then he punched his first Iraqi in the face, and pushed his first Iraqi down the stairs.---[back home] he was "crying and telling his wife---, 'I feel like a monster.'" [13] No Sir, the monster is the one who sent you there.

There are the thousands of vets who struggle with "PTS" daily and somehow manage to get to the next day. There are thousands of vets with estranged or lost personal relationships. There are thousands of vets who are homeless.

William Boardman, five-term elected sitting judge and distinguished author, tells about a group of veterans going to the VA headquarters "to talk to officials there about veteran suicides, veteran homelessness, veteran joblessness, and other veteran struggles. No one from the department would talk to them." [14]

Shameless, shameless, shameless VA! I'm sure you have your side of the story, and part of it would probably be that you are woefully understaffed because Congress starves you of funds. [15] So shame on Congress, too!

The Executive Addiction
Agencies in Supporting Roles

The U.S. is so deeply entrenched in warring and spying that I suspect there are few if any agencies not listed in Appendix C that should be listed for at least their indirect supporting roles. Two unlisted agencies that immediately come to mind are the U.S. Information Agency with its ties to the CIA and its disinformation favoring U.S. imperialism, and the Internal Revenue Service that collects citizens' revenue for warring and spying.

We can't let off the hook the other two branches of government, however, so let's move on to them. Anyone who agrees with Mr. Branfman's indictment of the executive branch will likely feel the same way about the other two branches.

The Legislative Addiction

I have written extensively elsewhere about what I sometimes refer to as "The U.S. Corpgress" and "The Chambers of Ill Repute. [16] Here I will call it by its real name, Congress. I'm not going to spend much time on it here, but I will return to it occasionally throughout the rest of the book.

The final part of Appendix C is what I call the "Bureaucracy of Check$ and Imbalances" and "The Lost and Fund Departments." Depicted there is a crazy quilt hodgepodge of committees and subcommittees of mostly lawyers with enough seniority and industrial backing to bankroll the war and spy agencies and to fake oversight of them.

The "public service" of interest here by the members of those committees and subcommittees is their getting and staying elected; making laws to legalize the habits; funding the government's habits; and "overseeing" the habits of the executive branch.

Getting and Staying Elected

To get elected and reelected to Congress is a very costly pursuit, and the candidates with the most money invariably win. So campaign financing is the key to the office. That is hardly a secret (although the givers and takers would like to keep it a secret).

Politicians campaign for office by tacitly promising once in office to favor wealthy self-interest groups that richly finance their campaigns. Does the thought of "bribery" enter your mind? If you follow the money trail as the authors of "The People's Business" have, you will see, they say, that a "pattern of influence will inevitably emerge" when major votes on issues affecting particular industries are compared to the campaign money and follow-up lobbying by those industries. [17]

How could this pattern not emerge? Would any sane person think corporations finance campaigns as a way to strengthen democracy and not themselves? If there were no issues, no huge profits, and no political careers at stake, you can take money to the bank there would be much less money for corporations and their lobbyists and much less job security for politicians. An indirect benefit to corporations incidentally, is that donations to politicians, particularly to the political careerists (and who in Congress isn't?) buoy share price by giving comfort and assurance to shareholders of politically favored corporations. [18]

Mike Masnick, an editor and entrepreneur, has written about just how much it "cost to win election to Congress" in the 2012 cycle. [19] "Both major political parties," he wrote, "have set up phone banks across the street from the Capitol (because it's seen as demeaning to do the calls directly from your Congressional office), and members of the House and the Senate spend a ridiculous amount of time there" hustling money for their re-election campaign. [20] One U.S. Senator calls it "dialing for dollars," and "Nothing," he says, "dominates the life of a senator more than raising money." [21]

According to Mr. Masnick, House members hustled on the average $1,689,580 each and Senators on the average $10,476,451 each. [22] I didn't do the math from those figures because I simply learned elsewhere that for the 2012 election cycle campaign contributions from all industries to candidates for Congress and the White House totaled about $6.2 billion. [23] A sizeable portion of the money paid for expensive advertising costs charged by the corporatized TV media that freely and very profitably uses airwaves that should be publicly owned and operated.

In the same 2012 election cycle the "defense" industry spent a total of about $27 million on campaign financing. [24] It is relatively small amount compared to the other industries' contributions, but the reason is simple. The other industries don't have as many other ways (discussed in the next chapter) to capture politicians. Nevertheless, the politicians know they can't take the war and spy industries completely for granted and so they are constantly holding fundraising events. [25] Moreover, over time the contributions continue to mount, with nearly $200 million having been spent since 1990. [26]

Being the secretive spy industry that it is makes it next to impossible to find out how much money that industry has spent on campaign contributions on any given election cycle. At a minimum the amount would start at $9.7 million. That's how much of a slush fund Senator Diane Feinstein, Chair of the Senate Intelligence Committee got for the 2012 election cycle. [27] That's a hefty contribution, but totally understandable because of her influential position. She's certainly not the exception, though. One reason members of Congress salivate over getting an influential committee assignment is because of that sluice fund.

To her total would need to be added the contributions to other key members of Congress. One of them, Mike Rogers, Chair of the House Intelligence Committee, received over $60 thousand in contributions for the same election cycle. This is the person who said on television; "You can't have your privacy violated if you don't know about it." [28] Mind you, he's the House Chair of Spying! Oh, I almost forgot. Among the other members are Mo, Dutch, Buck, and Bill reminiscent of the Marx Brothers. No, seriously, I'm not kidding. [29]

Any doubts about what the spy business gets in return for its campaign finance spending ought to be erased by just this one fact: "Lawmakers who upheld NSA phone spying received double the defense industry cash." That fact's description happens to be the title of an article. [30]

And so the true tale of money in politics goes on and on. Follow the money and you will find a politician in office or wanting to get there. I imagine you get the point and don't need any more data because I'm worn out finding what I did find.

Legislating the Habits

Congress does everything in its power and connives in secrecy to legislate U.S. warring and spying so as to make it legal (White House and agency lawyers can be counted on to pitch in and help in misinterpreting pesky laws that somehow got passed).

This is where the true story of the "touts" comes in. Touts are what Winston Churchill called lobbyists. When any of them comes through a Capitol Hill door the public's interest in getting legislation and budget allocations for the common good gets thrown out the window.

There are so many touts (over 11,000) that when they attend public hearings they pay "line sitters" who are law school students, bicycle messengers, even the homeless, to camp out overnight to get tickets in the Chamber's galleries. [31] Seems kind of silly and unnecessary to me. The hearings are just for show. By the time an issue of real significance gets a public hearing, the touts behind the scenes have already ghost written legislative drafts and their pawns are committed to them.

Lobbying is a follow up to the tacit bribery on the campaign trail. The follow up doesn't come cheaply, but it is money smartly spent by the industry and its touts. Would you believe, for instance, that the return on

102

investment (ROI) in lobbying by the pharmaceutical industry has been estimated at a mindboggling 77,500% on just one issue, barring the government from bargaining for cheaper drug prices through Medicare? [32] I have never ever seen reported such a huge percentage on anything else, let alone on industrial investments. I could find no comparable data for the war and spy industries but we can be sure their ROI is nothing to sneeze at or they wouldn't be spending the money on lobbying. Witness the aforementioned case of lawmakers protecting NSA.

In recent years over $3 billion has been spent annually by lobbyists swarming the halls and offices of Capitol Hill. Those lobbyists obviously aren't there on behalf of what the public needs from "public servants." They are there to keep and expand their clients' profits and to maximize their ROI's on lobbying by doing three things: writing draft legislation favoring their industries; making sure Congress funds warring and spying and protects those funds in times of "cutbacks," and telling the war and spy agencies what to buy.

The six industries most reckless with life (the war industry, the spy industry, the agribusiness industry, the pharmaceutical industry, the energy industry, and the firearms industry) spent almost half of the lobbying expenses of all 20 industries combined in 2012. [33] The closest I could come to a figure on lobbying expenses of the warring and spying industries for the year 2013 was over $57.7 million for the "defense aerospace industry." [34] That figure surely leaves out some of the lobbying expenses by the spying industry.

Funding the Habits

For the year 2013 the habits' budget was $1.3 trillion, over one-half the entire discretionary budget for the entire U.S. government. And if my calculations are correct, the habits' budget is 67 times greater than the combined budgets of all 50 states. Does that prove that the anti-federalists were right about opposing a strong central government during the debate over writing the U.S. Constitution? I think all of us who are opposed to America's warring and spying would think the proof is in the war and spy pudding. I can't imagine the 50 states and their citizens would have ever agreed to pool their money and people to create enemies around the world.

That is the short and long woeful story of 535 members of Congress throwing money left and right to sustain the two habits with eyes, ears, and conscience closed to the real needs of America.

"Overseeing" the Executive's Habits

Recall the two people sitting in the Chairs of House and Senate Spying and what keeps them sitting on those influential chairs. Does that tell you something about whether Congress "oversees" or "overlooks" the executive's habits? [35] The war and spy business spends a lot of money keeping their kind of people in those chairs muzzled and blindfolded except to the industrial benefactors. And their kind of people, some of whom also invest their own money in spying and warring contractors, are not about to tell the executive branch to crack down on both branches' benefactors. It's all a "mutual lifeline society."

The Judicial Addiction: SCOTUS

*Never have I urged impeachment of
Supreme Court justices. I do so now, for the
sake of ending the Supreme Court's
corporate-judicial dictatorship that is not
accountable under our system of checks
and balance in any other way.*
                              ---Ralph Nader [36]

*Lady Justice isn't blindfolded and her
scales aren't balanced.*
                              ---The author

The Supreme Court of the United States is the nation's so-called "court of last resort." That means it can make dreadful mistakes that millions of people affected adversely by it must live with unless SCOTUS later reverses itself. And the "robed injustices" have indeed made dreadful mistakes over the years that have impaired and enraged one group or another of our society. [37]

Cases involving America's warring and spying seldom rise to be heard by SCOTUS. The biased and compromised court rules in their favor of warring and spying when cases do arise. Here are three examples. SCOTUS supports U.S. wars; [38] SCOTUS doesn't like the CIA being embarrassed; [39] and SCOTUS supports military exercises over protection of marine species. [40]

The Judicial Addiction: Make-Believe Courts

It seems nothing legal can break the two habits while everything illegal sustain them. The government devilishly created two systems of "make-believe courts" to rubberstamp illegal warring and spying activities and to detain and punish military whistleblowers and suspected terrorists. One is the Foreign Intelligence Surveillance Court that rubberstamps requests from the spy agencies to do illegal spying. The other is the U.S. system of military tribunals and courts. It is a military tribunal that detains people at the Guantanamo encampment and allows them to be inhumanely treated, including that of torture. It was a military court that rendered such a harsh verdict on and sentencing of the whistleblower Bradley/Chelsea Manning.

Endnotes

1. Drawn partly from this trilogy of articles I wrote in 2012-2013: A Deadly Monster. An Overview of the Military-national Security, Industrial, Political triumvirate. Dissident Voice, December 11;. OpEdNews.com, December 12; An Outmatched Opposition. Dissident Voice, December 19, OpEdNews.com, December 31; 2012; and How the War Making Triumvirate might be "Pacified." OpEdNews.com, January 18; Dissident Voice, January 18., 2013.
2. The Efficacy and Ethics of U.S. Counterterrorism Strategy. Speech by John Q. Brennan at the Woodrow Wilson Center, April 30, 2012. www.wilsoncenter.org.
3. Brumback, G.B. An Unsent Letter to the President's Chief Counterterrorism Adviser. OpEdNews, May 17, 2012.
4. Branfman, F. World's Most Evil and Lawless Institution: Executive Branch of the U.S. Government? Dissident Voice, June 29, 2013.
5. Risen, C. Spies Among Us. The American Scholar, 2009, Winter Issue, 49. See also, Lichtblau, M. and Mazzetti, M. Military Expands Intelligence Role in U.S. New York Times, January 14, 2007.

6. See, e.g., my book, The Corpocracy and Megaliio's Turn Up Strategy. Palm Coast, FL: Democracy Power Press (Kindle Edition), 2012; and/or my six part series in 2013 on The Model Corporation: Introduction. Dissident Voice, February 26. OpEdNews.com, February 27; Shorter and Smaller are Better. Dissident Voice, February 28. OpEdNews, March1; Responsible Ownership, Governance, and Leadership. Dissident Voice, March 4; OpEdNews, March 5; An Uplifting Organizational Culture. Dissident Voice, March 5. OpEdNews, March 9; Managing Total Performance Properly. Dissident Voice, March 6. OpEdNews, March 11; and Up Against Ominous Realities. Dissident Voice, March 18. OpEdNews, March 18.

7. See, e.g., ACLU. Department of Homeland Security: Spying With No Direction. Undated; and Mueller, J. and Stewart, MG. Terror, Security, and Money: Balancing the Risks, Benefits, and Costs of Homeland Security. Paper presented at the Midwest Political Science Association, Chicago, IL, April 1, 2011.

8. Peterson, P. The U.S. Spends More on Defense than the Next Eight Countries Combined. Peter G. Peterson Foundation, April 13, 2014.

9. Benjamin, M. Don't Ask the Pentagon Where Its Money Goes. OpEdNews, October, 22, 2014.

10. Irwin, S. DoD Procurement Chief: Acquisition Programs Stuck in Cycle of Failure. NDIA Magazine, February 6, 2012.

11. Madrak, S. Soldier's Mom: Military Suicides Are 'Out of Control.' Crooks & Liars, November 27, 2012.

12. Staggenborg, R., MD. America's Post-traumatic Stress Disorder. OpEdNews, September 5, 2012.

13. Finkel, D. The Return: The Traumatized Veterans of Iraq and Afghanistan. The New Yorker, September 9, 2013, 36.

14. Boardman, W. What War Does to People. OpEdNews, November 13, 2012.

15. See, e.g., Staro, J. Ryan Seeking to Cut Already Underfunded VA Budget. Daily Kos, August 11, 2012.

16. See e.g., my articles written in 2014: The U.S. Corpgress. OpEdNews, January 16; and The Chambers of Ill Repute. Dissident Voice, January 30.

17. Drutman, L. & Cray, C. The People's Business: Controlling Corporations and Restoring Democracy. San Francisco: Berrett-Koehler, 2004, 220.

18. DeGroat, B. Corporate Political Donations Make Millions for Shareholders. News Service Online, January 24, 2007. See www.ur.umich.edu.

19. Masnick, M. How Much Does It Cost To Win Election To Congress? Tech Dirt, March 14, 2013.

20. Masnick, M. Ibid.

21. Packer, G. The Empty Chamber: Just How Broken is the Senate? The New Yorker, August 9, 2010, 38-51.

22. Masnick, M. Op cit.

23. Choma, R. The 2012 Election: Our Price Tag (Finally) for the Whole Ball of Wax. Open Secrets.org, March 13, 2013.

24. Novak, V. Defense Industry Campaign Influence and Lobbying. Center for Responsive Politics, August 2013.

25. McElhatton, J. Contractor Political Donations Unscathed by Sequester. Federal Times, March 22, 2013.

26. McElhatton, J. Ibid.

27. BallotPedia. Dianne Feinstein's Campaign Contribution History http://ballotpedia.org February 8, 2014.

28. Guariglia, M. Which NSA Defenders Take the Most Money from Defense Contractors? January 3, 2014. http://www.heavy.com/news/2014/01/nsa-contractors-money-dianne-feinstein-mike-rogers

29. Knefel, J. Meet Six Politicians Getting Rich from America's Endless Wars. AlterNet, February 21, 2013;

also, Sotile, JP. The Military-Industrial Marx Brothers. February 28, 2013 http://newsvandal.com/2013/02/the-military-industrial-marx-brothers

30. Kravets, D. Lawmakers Who Upheld NSA Phone Spying Received Double the Defense Industry Cash. Wired, July 26, 2013. www.wired.com

31. Murray, D. Corporate Lobbying: 'Line Sitters' Cash in on Quest for Influence. The Blade Online, December 7, 2003.

32. Jilani, Z. Big Pharma Gets 77,500% Return On Lobbying Investment. Republic.org, April 3, 2012.

33. See Open Secrets.org for lobbying data. http://www.opensecrets.org/

34. Open Secrets, Ibid.

35. Lizza, R. State of Deception: Why won't the President Rein in the Intelligence Community? The New Yorker, 2013, 50.

36. Nader, R. Time for Impeachment? The Corporate Supreme Court. Counterpunch, November 18, 2913.

37. Brumback, GB. Robed Injustice. OpEdNews, November 19; Dissident Voice, November 19; Cyrano's Journal, November 20; Uncommon Thought Journal, November 22, 2013.

38. Schlesinger v. Reservists Committee to Stop the War (No. 72-1188). Legal Information Institute, Cornell University Law School, June 25, 1974.

39. Snepp, F. Snowden and a Muzzled Free Press. Special to CNN.com, July 3, 2013.

40. Legal Information Institute. Winter v. Natural Resource Defense Council Inc.,November12, 2008.

CHAPTER 5
THE ADDICTED WAR AND SPY INDUSTRIES

The War Contractors
Makers of Industrial Weapons That Kill, Maim, and Destroy

During the American Revolution George Washington had to rely on a ragtag army and ragtag sources of supplies, the most critical of which was the musket. Some muskets were supplied by local gunsmiths, some by European manufacturers, and some from dead British soldiers.
Today his 44th successor has at his command the largest arsenal in the world provided by the largest number of war contractors in the world. A list of the 100 largest ones is shown in Appendix D. (there are probably thousands of smaller contractors and subcontractors). It would be impossible but also unnecessary in this one book to profile every contractor on that list. It took one book to write in some detail about just one of them. [1] That contractor is the first of just three to be sketched momentarily. We won't be missing anything noteworthy by my not including more sketches (most of the data in the sketches are based on information retrieved from the Internet in 2014).

While some of the contractors may not make and peddle lethal weapons (e.g., Johns Hopkins University presumably doesn't), in one way or another they are all in the war business, and they all depend on our government creating and keeping foreign enemies. Some of the war contractors, as you can see, have also become spy contractors, and at least one has gotten into the health care business. What this tells us is that if the war and spy money dried up and peace money were available these contractors with their versatile skills ought to be able to figure out how to follow the peace money by making and peddling peace products (see the last chapter about giving them a helping hand in this conversion).

Lockheed Martin

Lockheed Martin is the most costly, the most powerful, the most profitable, and the largest, defense contractor in the world. It has cost the taxpayers around a quarter of a trillion dollars in just 10 years; its annual arms sales are over $35 billion; its total profit around $3 billion; over 132,000 people are dependent directly for a livelihood on this behemoth employer. [2]

Like all the rest on the list in Appendix D Lockheed Martin knows how to buy and manipulate the federal government. It places through the revolving door key people in influential government positions; its political campaign contributions over the years total more than $25 million; and its lobbying expenditures over the years total more than $172 million.

Buying and plying politicians help explain why this defense contractor continues to do business with Uncle Sam even while being high on a list of instances of misconduct by defense contractors (the list covers cases of contract fraud and environmental, ethics, and labor violations). [3] If you and I had even a small fraction of those violations you know where we would be living.

Lockheed Martin is also a very much diversified corporation and what else it does besides make and sell deadly weapons may make it a unique defense contractor. It sorts the mail but is not the USPS; cuts Social Security checks but is not the SSA; counts the census but is not the Bureau of the Census; monitors air traffic; but is not the FAA; runs space flights but is not NASA; and helps spy on Americans but is not NSA. [4] This seems to be no ordinary defense contractor. But what follows is a true story about "Herk" that exemplifies how Lockheed Martin does business that's not out of the ordinary for the industry or for other industries.

Meet the "Herk"

"Herk" is my nickname for the C-130 Hercules, a mid-sized transport airplane first designed and built in the 1950s (it's so big it could also be nicknamed the "Hulk"). The author of the article about it tells us to "consider this a parable to help us see past the alarmist talking points issued by defense contractor lobbyists, the public relations teams they hire, and the think tanks they fund. It may help us see just how effective defense contractors are in growing their businesses, whatever the mood of the moment." [5]

The mood in the late 1970s for Herk and its maker was anxiety over the future of its sales. The Pentagon had decided that it didn't need any more Herks and stopped asking Congress for any more of them. This decision had followed two earlier setbacks for the defense contractor. One, the Air Force awarded a lucrative contract to a competitor but Congress gave the loser, Lockheed Martin, a bailout of about $1 billion in loan guarantees and other financial relief. The other was having been caught using some of the bailout money to bribe foreign officials to buy Herks.

It was a needless worry. The contractor knew reflexively what to do next. It ignored the Pentagon and by giving more campaign money to key Congressional members up for reelection and then bombarding them with lobbyists got Congress to earmark money for more Herks. Not content to settle for just that sweet deal, the contractor next collaborated with advocacy groups of local Air Force Reserves and Air National Guard to lobby governors and Congress to keep bases scheduled for closing open for the surplus Herks, to argue for even more Herks, and to keep the older ones from being mothballed.

The story of Herk is a never ending one. The contractor recently sold a bundle of the planes to the Royal Saudi Air Force, and the Pentagon apparently now has a hankering for a more modernized version of Herk. This is indeed a plane that continues to enrich the contractor and rob the taxpayer.

And the F35

I don't want to finish this vignette without mentioning Herk's sibling, the F35, reportedly the most expensive military weapons program in US history. Not at all atypical performance in the industry, the contractor's projected cost of $226 billion for 2900 planes and a fly date of 2012 has since become $400 billion for 500 fewer planes with a fly date delayed to 2017. The Pentagon's plan to terminate part of the shoddy program was thwarted by the contractor marching up Capitol Hill to lobby the House Armed Services Committee. [6]

Imagine what might happen if a lobbying association, let's call it True Patriots for America, sent five million people to Washington demanding that the government cut the defense/intelligence budget to the bone and reorient U.S. foreign policy to building friendships with all other nations (the Department of Homeland Security might roll out the thousands of tanks it bought to meet the True Patriots).

We may never see the end of the F35 either. As recently as early 2014 the Pentagon "repeatedly waived laws banning Chinese-built components on U.S. weapons in order to keep the $392 billion Lockheed Martin Corp F-35 fighter program on track in 2012 and 2013, even as U.S. officials were voicing concern about China's espionage and military buildup." [7]

Recall the War Resistors League's examples of what could have been done constructively with the money spent just on the Iraq war. Hayes Brown, an editor and writer, has also given us some tabulated examples of lost opportunity costs not from money wasted on a war but on the F35, the plane that can't fly: every schoolchild in America could have been fed; every homeless American could have been bought a mansion; every humanitarian crisis could have been funded unilaterally; security could have been provided around the world; and substantial funding needed to rebuild America could have been made available. [8]

Northrop Grumman

This defense contractor is among the largest in the world; has net annual earnings of around $24 billion; employs over 122,000 worldwide; is a big campaign contributor and big lobbyist; has paid picayune fines for defrauding the government; is fourth on the contractor misconduct list, and, of course, keeps on getting government contracts. [9]

Meet Global Hawk

I chose this contractor so as to tell the story of its Global

Hawk. It is simply a different weapon in the sky made by a different member of the industry. It's yet another case study of a different defense contractor's clout in Washington at America's expense. Global Hawk has been called the "huge drone that could not be grounded." [10]

Like the F35, "Global Hawk" had cost far more than projected and was riddled with flaws. The Air Force, with an anxious eye on possible budget cuts planned to clip the wings of the costly and hobbled bird. You can guess what Northrop Grumman did in response. It's a natural reflex for defense contractors: Race up to Capitol Hill and save the bird! Indebted to the contractor for their political careers members of Congress reflexively obliged, saving the bird while costing taxpayers another $2.5 billion over five years.

An authoritative analyst of the industry observed that Northrop Grumman's political strategy "is entirely predictable — hire the right people, target the right people, contribute to the right people, then link them together with subcontractors and go for the gold. Killing a major program, in production, is rather like vampire-killing. You have to drive a silver stake through its heart to make sure it is dead." [11]

General Dynamics

General Dynamics is among the oldest (its roots are in the late 19th century) and five largest defense contractors in the world with net annual earnings around $32 billion. It employs over 70,000 people worldwide. It is a big campaign contributor and big lobbyist. [12] It was once named the "War Profiteer of the Month." [13] It is a recidivist defrauder of the government that gets slaps on the wrist and, of course, gets continued contracts. [14] Its executives spin through the revolving doors of the military/industrial/political triumvirate like its one big cozy family. [15]

It has also invested heavily in and profited immensely from adding spy contractor on its resume. "There's no better place to start than---General Dynamics," wrote two investigative reporters, to understand how contractors have exploited the 9/11 tragedy. They quote a company spokesman, ""The American intelligence community is an important market for our company. Over time, we have tailored our organization to deliver affordable, best-of-breed products and services to meet those agencies' unique requirements." [16] Well, it's only affordable because taxpayers have to shell out the dough, and being "best-breed" isn't saying much in a shoddy industry.

I have been tracking this war/spy contractor for decades, much, much, longer than any of the other contractors, and long before it got into the lucrative spying business. What drew me to it was my early interest and research on human values and ethics. I have written several case studies about it and summarize them here.

Case Study of General Dynamics: Paper Ethics

After allegedly repeated and egregious wrongdoing, General Dynamics finally got a directive from the government in 1985 barring the company from further business orders until it established a compliance program. [17] The company quickly responded by retaining an ethics consulting firm to draft an ethics code (every corporation has one); creating an ethics committee of outsiders to serve on the board of directors; hiring an outsider to be the corporate ethics program director;

116

holding ethics workshops for employees; and opening a hotline for whistleblowers.

The ban was lifted in three months (Uncle Sam needs its war products). The ethics program director was honored in a feature article of a professional journal in which he was quoted as advising companies to "do a few things very well because only a few things really need to be done." [18]

Well, not exactly, Mr. Ethics Program Director. While a compliance program may help a company meet its contractual and other legal obligations, it can't help put a company on higher moral ground, and may even perpetuate wrongdoing by giving the company a false sense of immunity. General Dynamics is a case in point. I tracked publicity about the contractor for several years following its heralded compliance program. Among the reported misdeeds were low balling bids, violation of safety regulations; a bonus plan for the top 25 managers deemed "just outrageous" by a government official; and, in the last file entry (before I went on to other matters), giving a 10-year employee a layoff notice the very day the employee returned from bereavement leave following the death of the employee's young son. [19]

Case Study of General Dynamics: Website PR

Not long ago I browsed General Dynamics' website (I see that its content has changed somewhat since then). There was a picture of a "Stryker armored combat vehicle" that was used heavily in the Iraq war (add bells and whistles to a tank, give it a new name and make a killing). Under the picture was this caption, "STRENGTH ON YOUR SIDE" "We adhere to the highest standards of conduct and ethics." I was then directed to click on "About Our

Ethics." Before going there, stop and think a moment about the sheer hype and falsity of what I saw. There is absolutely nothing ethical about a combat tank and everything immoral and murderous. Moreover, the implication that there's "peace through strength" is sheer PR and BS.

I then "clicked" to see more: "At General Dynamics, we know each day our employees will make decisions that are critical to our success [as a war profiteer]. To help ensure those decisions meet our company's ethical standards, General Dynamics' Board of Directors and management have devoted significant time and resources to maintaining an active and robust ethics program."

I looked at what that program was: 13 business unit ethics officers and 120 local ethics officers who implement the ethics program by carrying out a list of seven responsibilities that include distributing the ethics handbook (every corporation has one); provision of "a 24-hour-a-day, seven-day- a-week, confidential Business Ethics Helpline-callers may remain anonymous if they wish (they sure as H--- better); and "conducting and overseeing prompt, thorough and objective investigations of all reported allegations of suspected ethical misconduct and taking corrective action, if necessary."

Déjà Vu. Does all this remind you of the first case study? Has General Dynamics been implicated in fraud cases since its ethics program was touted nearly 30 years ago? In 1990 it settled (paying a meager $8 million fine) a government lawsuit charging the company with defrauding the Army on contracts for M-1 tanks. In the mid-1990s there were indications that General Dynamics had bribed the South Korean president to facilitate a deal to spend $5 billion on the company's F-16 fighter jets. In

118

2004 it and General Motors signed a consent agreement to settle charges that they violated the Arms Export Control Act through the unauthorized export of technical data and defense services. In 2008 its Electric Boat subsidiary signed a consent order with the state of Connecticut and paid $75,000 to settle violations relating to the discharge of pollutants into the Thames River. In 2008 a Congressional committee blamed poor management by the Defense Department and General Dynamics for billions of dollars in cost overruns and delays in a Marine Corps tank program. [20] In 2008 General Dynamics settled for $4 million for fraudulently overbilling the Navy. [21]

Has General Dynamics been whistle clean since 2008? Well, I see that it is still on the contractor misconduct list, and it hasn't stopped its war profiteering. [22] And it won't stop until our government stops its war making.

Case Study of General Dynamics: It Takes One to Know One

General Dynamics has gotten into the business of helping organizations "combat healthcare fraud, waste and abuse (FWA)." In its website, the company says "With STARSSolutions Suite, we can help you discern innocent errors from outright fraudulent intent. No other solution in the marketplace provides the same level of detection, automation, in-depth analysis, integrated workflow and ROI. It can serve as a powerful tool in decreasing FWA losses, increasing recoveries, developing provider educational programs, and optimizing operational efficiencies. We can help you augment your fraud, waste and abuse detection and investigation activities through our highly experienced Special Investigations Unit team." [23]

Need more be said? Enough is enough. Let's move on to the spy business.

The Spy Contractors

In the second part of Appendix D is a list of some spy contractors significant enough to get noticed. It's a surprisingly small list, but there apparently are thousands of contractors snooping around. It's impossible given the nature of their business for me to know precisely just how many there really are. But why should I apologize? The Director of National Intelligence doesn't even know who his agency's "core" intelligence contractors are! [24] Makes one wonder how many of his "peripheral" contractors have been lost in the underground maze of moles.

Most of the spy contractors on the list may not be exactly household names, but one of them, Booze, Allen and Hamilton became an instant household name when its former employee, whistleblower Edward Snowden, leaked revealing information about snooping by the NSA. Amazon, of course, is a household name but you might have been surprised to see it on the list. It's there because its "cloud" technology for handling massive spy data was wanted badly enough by the CIA that it forked over more than one-half billion dollars in a contract with Amazon, which reportedly has had a "bad history of currying favor with the U.S. government's "national security" establishment." [25] Then there's Google. Millions of people use it but may not know it has a contract with a spy in the sky agency, the National Geospatial-Intelligence Agency. [26]

I have not gone to the effort to research and sketch some illustrative spy contractors like I did the war contractors.

120

Spy contractors don't like the sunlight, and I'm not about to prowl around in the dark looking for details about particular spies. In their business, the Devil is not in the details but in the mere existence of the business. Instead, what I will do is a take a composite "mug shot" of them, as if we had just booked them in a holding cell for behavior against freedom, against privacy, and, oh, against a true democracy.

Their mug shot is no different really than that of the war contractors, particularly the ones that have also gotten into the spying business. [27] Like the war contractors to a great extent, spy contractors:

> buy influential politicians' offices for them
> swarm Capitol Hill with touts
> go through the revolving door
> profit immensely from government contracts
> give their CEOs spy high compensation
> defraud the government and still get lucrative contracts.
> flout any law in the way
> vastly outnumbers government's own spies
> cost twice as much to spy as government's own spies
> get Top Secret clearances for nearly one-half million people
> need to rely on hundreds of recruiting firms for new hires

Bringing Home the Caviar

The last bulleted item about needing hundreds of recruiting firms does not mean contractors in the two industries are known as a "job of last resort." It simply means the demand has outstripped the supply. Get that job and start bringing home the caviar, so to speak.

Let's start with CEO caviar. The average compensation package for CEOs of the top five DoD contractors was a stratospheric $21.5 million in 2011. [28] These fat cats better stay where they are. Their industry-specific know-how isn't readily transferable. [29] The government doesn't have the nerve to cap CEO compensation, but the cap placed on the rest of the contractor work force is around $800 thousand, a "mere sub stratospheric" amount, maybe enough for caviar not daily but weekly. [30] The contractors' janitors probably don't bring home caviar but I bet they are better paid than all other janitors.

The War and Spy Contractors' "Owners"

"Members of the Profit before Honor Owners' Club" may be the world's largest club unless there's one for the poor. Guess how many members of Congress belong to this "owners'" club? The last time I looked the number was 151 shareholders, but that figure is more than five years old. [31] We could safely add 50 or more by now I should think.

The two industries yield very good ROI's (return on investments) if you aren't squeamish about investing in merchants of misery and death. And thousands upon thousands of investors aren't. A writer for Forbes magazine gives five reasons why other sectors are not as good an investment as is the defense industry sector: its stocks weather economic storms better; it dominates the market "selling Uncle Sam a billion dollars in goods and services every day, seven days a week;" it is "politically protected" (that's an understatement); its oblivious to any "waning demand;" and its future prospects are more publicly known through news of any impending dips in the defense budget and thus give cautious investors pause to reconsider." [32]

We can partly blame the "owners" for the consequences of their companies' warring and spying but we can't sue them for death and other damages. The reason why dates back over two centuries ago in America's history when the first state in the union enacted a limited liability law and other states quickly followed suit in a race to the bottom. States initially gave their chartered corporations limited liability only if they provided public services, but with the advent of sham charters, any chartered corporation gets limited liability. That includes the chartered and insulated war and spy contractors.

The Chariot before the Horse
How the Two Industries Dictate to Uncle Sam

Let's count the ways: five. The two overlapping industries, not the American people at large, tell their government what its annual war/security budget should be, what its war/security purchases should be, for what purposes, and how much they should cost, and what minimal legislation and oversight would be acceptable. These industries exercise this stranglehold in several ways. Some of them we have already mentioned.

1. The Two Industries Get their Pawns and Patrons Elected

The industries donate millions of dollars in campaign contributions. The main focus is always to ensure that members of Congressional committees important to these two industries get reelected.

2. The Two Industries Strategically Locate their Facilities

The industries' lifelines and profit bonanzas come from contracts awarded by influential and courted members of Congress. Locating facilities in their Congressional districts and States helps ensure that contracts will be steered to them. Few things make a member of Congress more anxious than the prospect of a facility moving out or a member more pleased than a facility moving in. If I'm not mistaken there are one or more military and/or spy contractor facilities in every state of the union. I call it the "spread your employment security blanket."

3. The Two Industries Swarm Capitol Hill with their Touts

In one year alone millions of dollars were spent to send about 1,000 touts up Capitol Hill to cash in on all those campaign financing bribes from the sector by telling their elected officials to keep boosting the federal budget for the sector, what and how to legislate and regulate the sector's business, and to peddle its products and supplies. Trade associations are clusters of touts concentrating on a particular kind of war/security business and thus represent not one but all of the corporations in that business. These associations include the Aerospace Industries Association, Armed Forces Communications Electronics Association, Association for Unmanned Vehicle Systems, Intelligence and National Security Alliance, International National Defense Industrial Association (INSA), and the Submarine Industrial Base Council.

By the way, want to know a funny story about INSA? Two days after publishing a paper on cyber security the top spy trade association discovered its website was hacked. [33] I imagine it's embarrassing, not funny to INSA.

4. The Two Industries' Representatives Come and Go Through the Revolving Door

Now you see them here. Now you see them there. Who are they and where are they coming and going? They don't stay put like the career bureaucrats do. They are the self-serving shufflers back and forth through the so-called, perfectly named "revolving door." The war and spy agencies and contractors are no different from the rest of the shufflers throughout America's corpocracy.

There are actually three sets of revolving doors. One is for industry executives and lobbyists who go through to appointments in key government posts to ensure industry interests aren't denied by the American people. There's the government-to-industry door through which public officials, having gotten experience and valuable contacts from the inside in keeping public interests at bay, go to the industry and parlay their experience and contacts into furthering industry interests in exchanges, usually private, with the government. And finally, there's the government-to-lobbyist door through which former legislators, their staffs, and executive-branch officials pass on the way to lucrative positions in lobbying firms to lobby their former colleagues.

5. The Two Industries Give Politicians Junket Trips and Other Goodies

Congressional members vital to the two industries are plied with junkets to sunny places in the winter, honored with awards, and in other ways to cater to their egos, palates and pleasures. For example, the Aerospace

Industries Association in 2011 handed one of its top awards, the Wings of Liberty, to Sen. Patty Murray (D-Wash.), one of the co-chairmen of the special deficit-cutting committee. The award was given to her, not coincidentally, "on the same day the congressional super committee held its first public business meeting," presumably to influence her vote on any budget cut that would hurt that Association's industrial interests. [34]

A Marriage Made in Hell
A True Story of Drone Lovers

This true story about a drone trade show illustrates quite well I think the flow of money and favors between government and industry.

If the two were not tied together at the groin and all parts above and below, you would expect the show to be held at a private facility, like say, a big arena rented by the "Association for Unmanned Vehicle Systems International (AUVSI). But this is a true story, not fiction.

The event, publicly masked as a "science fair," was held in the large foyer of the Rayburn House Office building adjacent to Capitol Hill. The host was the U.S. House Unmanned Systems Caucus (USUMSC), a bunch of politicians who care more about robots than people, except of course, themselves and their kind of people. I'm not sure which name came first, but I would guess that AUVSI did and then convinced "the industry's man on Capitol Hill" ---to start an Unmanned Systems Caucus---." And as fast as a knee jerk its members have since been "showered ---with cash."

Hawkers "in suits, polo shirts or military garb" from companies like those listed in Appendix D were showing "the hottest new drones, robots and mini blimps." Well, they weren't the real thing obviously, just toy replicas.

The author of this story, John Amick, director of Brave New World Foundation's "War Costs" project, concluded the story with this witty remark, "The toy du jour for this [marriage] is the drone. New technology, same game." [35] And the game is endless. A trade show for each new toy. The story John told was just his "drone edition."

Who is getting more screwed than the marriage of drone lovers who never get out of bed? You got it, the taxpayers who are not even in the house, let alone in the bedroom. Truth is indeed stranger and definitely more deadly and costly than fiction. End of this story but not quite the end of this chapter.

The Race to Hell

Drones are just one of the newer deadly toys on the market (that we know about). How much does a drone cost Uncle Sam now days? The priciest drone may be the Global Hawk, the one you met pages ago (and fortunately not by its flying over your house). It "only" costs around $140 million a drone. That's piddling compared to the $2 billion price tag for one battleship.

Drones and battleships, of course, are just two in a cornucopia of different kinds of weapons made by America's weapon makers and sold not only for the U.S. military but also for foreign nations that get the weapons directly from the U.S. government and also directly from US weapons makers licensed to sell and export their weapons directly. I bet the license agreements and the government monitoring of them are so porous and lax that war companies have a free hand to sell to the highest bidders or to any and all bidders.

The U.S. is second only to Russia in arms trade. Business Insider reports that for the year 2013 Russia exported $27.9 billion worth of weapons while the US exported $26.9 billion. [36] The two Super Powers together put killer weapons in the hands of 74 different regimes, mostly those among the developing nations. Joining in the arms race but farther behind in exporting weapons are France, United Kingdom, Germany, China,, Italy and assorted other countries. [37] Hanging over these figures like a mushroom cloud are nuclear weapons possessed by nine or so nations. [38]

These data are not just cold statistics; they are terrifying realities if you think about the implications. Just think, for example, that there are potential powder kegs in nearly one-half of the world's sovereign states. If not doused those kegs could eventually inflame the world (see my Armageddon scenario in Chapter 8). Weapons in the hands of madmen do not stay shelved.

Endnotes

1. Hartung, W. Prophets of War: Lockheed Martin and the Making of the Military-Industrial Complex. Nation Books, 2010.
2. Wikipedia, www.wikipedia.org/wiki/Lockheed_Martin; and Weigley, S. 10 companies Profiting the Most from War. 24/7 Wall St.,March 10, 2013.
3. Freeman, B. Ex Lockheed Lobbyist Now in Key Defense Oversight Role. The Project on Government Oversight Blog, July 26, 2012.Project on Government Oversight. Federal Contractor Data Base. December 26, 213.www.contractormisconduct.org;Influence explorer. LockheedMartin.2012. www.influenceexplorer.com.
4. See www.lockheedmartin.com; Hartung, W.D. Is Lockheed Martin Shadowing You? How a Giant Weapons

Maker Became the New Big Brother. TomDispatch.com, January 11, 2011.

5. Goulka, J. Lockheed Martin's Herculean Lobbying Efforts, Mother Jones, March 11, 2013.

6. Van Dorn, M. Lockheed Martin No Stranger To Ethically Questionable Lobbying. Truthful Lobbying, June 24, 2013.

7. Shiffman, J. and Shalal-Esa, A. Exclusive: U.S. Waived Laws to Keep F-35 on Track with China-made Parts. Reuters, January 3, 2014.

8. Brown, H. Americans Have Spent Enough Money On A Broken Plane To Buy Every Homeless Person A Mansion. Think Progress, July10, 2014..

9. See www.wikipedia.org/wiki/Northrop_Grumman; Weigley, S. 10 Ccompanies Profiting the Most from War. 24/7 Wall St. ,March 10, 2013; and Project on Government Oversight. Federal Contractor Data Base. www.contractormisconduct.org, December 26, 2013.

10. Sia, RHP & Cohen, A. The Huge Drone That Could Not Be Grounded. The Center for Public Integrity, July 16, 2013.

11. Op. cit.

12. See www.wikipedia.org/wiki/General_Dynamics; www.opensecrets.org; Weigley, S. 10 Companies Profiting the Most from War. 24/7 Wall St. , March 10, 2013.

13. War Resisters' International. War Profiteer of the Month: General Dynamics. http://www.wri-irg.org/node/318, February 1, 2008.

14. David Wood. Pentagon Reports Billions of Dollars in Contractor Fraud. HuffPost Politics, December 16, 2011.

15. Mulvany, L. Lobbyists for General Dynamics Who Passed through the Revolving Door. Center for Public Integrity, July 30, 2012.

16. Priest, D. & Arkin, WM. National Security Inc. Washington Post, September, 2011.

17. Buckley, W.F. The Defense Bilkers. The Washington Post, August 20, 1985.

18. W. H. Wagel. A New Focus on Business Ethics at General Dynamics. Personnel, 1987, 64: pp. 4-8.

19. Dwyer, P. & Payne, S. "The General Dynamics Case Sets a Bad Precedent", Business Week, June 8, 1987, 41; Ellis, J. E. & Payne, S. "More Instant Cash than a Lottery: Under GD's Plan, Managers Get a Windfall-and Shareholders Get Ulcers." Business Week, May 20, 1991, 42; Lawrence, M. OSHA Fines Shipbuilder $615,000, The Washington Post, July 30, 1987, E1-2; and Marshall, S. "After Son's Death, a Pink Slip for Dad", USA TODAY, March 26, 1993, 3A.

20. These transgressions were reported by Phil Mattera. General Dynamics. Crocodyl.org (the corporate malfeasance wiki of Corporatewatch.org)

21. Reuters. General Dynamics Settles Navy Fraud Case at $4 Mln. August 18, 2008.

22. Project on Government Oversight. Federal Contractor DataBase.December26,2013. www.contractormisconduct.org

23. Meudt, M. General Dynamics Announces Solutions to Stop Healthcare Fraud Next-Generation STARS Solutions Anti-fraud Software Will Help Curb Improper Healthcare Costs. General Dynamics Press Release, November 17, 2009.

24. Wong, K. Report: Intelligence community can't keep track of its contractors. The Hill.com, February 13, 2014.

25. Solomon, N. Under Amazon's CIA Cloud: The Washington Post, December 18, 2013.

26. Wohltman, S. and Dixon, P. Google Earth Builder Supports NGA Geospatial Efforts. Google Enterprise Blog, April 20, 2011.

27. Spy contractors are represented in some of the sources already cited for the war contractors. Some additional sources: Brown, H. What You Should Know About The

Intelligence Community's Contractors. ThinkProgress, June 10, 2013; O'Harrow Jr., R., Priest, D.& Censer, M. Private Contractors Play Key Role in U.S. Intelligence Work. The Washington Post, June 12, 2013; Shaw, D. Intel Contractors Give Millions to Lawmakers Overseeing Government Surveillance. December 7, 2013; http://maplight.org/content; Shorrock, T. INSA – How Money and Power Corrupts National Security. June 9, 2013. http://timshorrock.com/?p=1822; and Shorrock, T. Meet the Contractors Analyzing your Private Data. Salon, June 10, 2013.

28. Freeman, B. Pentagon Contractor CEO Compensation is Second to None. The Project on Government Oversight, August 22, 2012.

29. Morgenson, G. C.E.O.'s and the Pay-'Em-or-Lose-'Em Myth. The New York Times, September 22, 2012.

30 .Brown, H. Report: Federal Defense Contractors Paid Almost Double Obama's Salary. Think Progress, June 24, 2013.

31. Mayer, LR. Congress Invested in Defense Contracts. Opensecrets, April 3, 2008.

32. Thompson, L. Five Reasons The Defense Industry Is Still A Better Investment Than Other Sectors. Forbes, September 10, 2012.

33. Lake, E. Top Spy Website Hacked. The Daily Beast, September 16, 2011.

34. Dayen, D. Defense Industry Gives Top Super Committee Democrat An Award. news.firedoglake.com, September 14, 2011.

35. Amick, J. When the Defense Industry and Congress are Indistinguishable: Drone Edition. September 14, 2012. http://www.warcosts.com.

36. Smith, A. & Gould, S. This Map of US and Russian Arms Sales Says It All. Business Insider, August 13, 2014.

37. Shah, A. The Arms Trade is Big Business. Global Issues, January 5, 2013.

38.Kimball, D. Nuclear Weapons: Who Has What at a Glance. Arms Control Association, June233, 2014.

CHAPTER 6
THE HABIT HELPERS

Banksters and War Street
Behavior Shapers
The Toy Industry
The Gun Industry
Science
Foreign Enemies
Bystanders

The warriors and spies in America are more powerful than any other known counterpart on earth. Their habits are well fortified. Yet they don't want to leave anything to chance. So they also depend on millions of "Habit Helpers." Who are they? I was once one of them. Let's take a brief look at them. Knowing who they are is a must if there is going to be any chance of breaking the habits. There are seven by name; the banksters, the behavior shapers, the toy industry, the gun industry, science, foreign enemies, and bystanders.

The Banksters and War Street

> *History records that the Money Changers have used every form of abuse, intrigue, deceit and violent means possible to maintain control over governments by controlling money and its issuance.*
> ---James Madison [1]

Permit me to issue and control a nation's money and I care not who makes the laws.
   ---Mayer Amschel Rothschild [2]

Whoever controls the volume of money in any country is absolute master of all industry and commerce.
   --- President James Garfield [3]

It is well that the people of the nation do not understand our banking and monetary system, for if they did, I believe there would be a revolution before tomorrow morning.
   ---Henry Ford [4]

Who controls money controls the world.
   ---Henry Kissinger [5]

And who has more money, controls the money and loans the money if not the banksters on War Street along with their big Mother Bank, the Federal Reserve and the international play makers such as The World Bank? Not the U.S. government! It's in debt, some $20 trillion worth, much of it war and spy debts. That amounts to a whole lot of interest Uncle Sam has to pay, and you know who gets theinterest.

When Ted Nace wrote his marvelous book, "Gangs of America," he was referring to corporate and government rogues. [6] He gave scant attention to the financial industry; Wall Street isn't even in his subject index. I can't do the same here. I must give it its due, no matter howbriefly.

"Banksters," of course, is a euphemism for gangsters, and,

134

if you know the "upbringing" of America, you know that bankers have had their acquisitive hands in that upbringing almost every step of the way, including causing along with laissez faire government numerous "downbringings," or economic depressions, with the last one being what I have called the "Economic Katrina" of 2008 that swept away Main Street while leaving War Street high and dry from government bailouts. [7]

> *All wars are bankers' wars!*
> ---Michael Rivero [8]

But the banksters haven't been content just to gamble with America's economy. They have been even more rapacious, conniving and reckless in goading, sometimes orchestrating, funding, and feeding on America's warring and imperialism from the late 19th century forward. The logic of their involvement I think is that they benefit doubly by protecting and expanding their global investments and power and by raking in profits from the government's war debts.

Name a war and there they were, not on the battlefield but safely behind the scenes counting their money. They were behind the Banana Wars. They protected with military help their investment in the construction of a cross-country canal in Nicaragua. A few years later, wanting to protect their interests in Cuba led them to push for and get the American-Spanish War. As time passed they had their hands in every noteworthy military intervention by the U.S. They promoted and financed America's involvement in WWI and WWII, where "the Morgans got their war in Europe, the Rockefellers theirs in Asia." [9] The banksters made sure they were not left out in the cold during the Cold War, or in any of the many other military episodes and killing sprees such as the Korean War, The Vietnam

War, the many coup d'états (e.g., Iran), The Iraq War, etc., etc.

The Banksters' Revolving Door

The war and spy industries and the other industries were not the first to go through the revolving door to influential political appointments and back. The banksters were the trend setters, starting possibly with Grover Cleveland's administration that was "honeycombed" with banksters and continuing to Obama's "Wall Street Cabinet." [10]

Misfits? Do the Banksters Belong in this Chapter?

On second thought, do the banksters really belong in this chapter instead of in their own as part of the war and spy complex? If they could have their way they would create a "new world order" in which they do the ordering and the world does their will. Read what the world's premier and wealthiest banker, David Rockefeller allegedly told fellow plutocrats at a meeting of the Trilateral Commission in 1991. [11]

> We are grateful to The Washington Post, The New York Times, Time Magazine and other great publications whose directors have attended our meetings and respected their promises of discretion for almost forty years. It would have been impossible for us to develop our plan for the world if we had been subject to the bright lights of publicity during those years. But, the work is now much more sophisticated and prepared to march towards a world government. The supranational sovereignty of an intellectual elite and world bankers is surely preferable
>
> to the national autodetermination practiced in past centuries.

136

Just imagine a world ruled by "intellectual elites" and "world bankers" who could always rely on America's regime and its two nasty habits to restore order if the new order got a bit shaky.

The Behavior Shapers

Power is in tearing human minds to pieces and putting them together again in new shapes of your own choosing.
> ---George Orwell [12]

Give me a child and I'll shape him into anything.
> ---B. F. Skinner [13]

Think tanks
Shams (NGOs/front groups)
Religion
Education
Mainstream media
PR industry

America's babies don't burst into life holding guns and wearing spy glasses. Some of them "shape" up to become warriors and spies and many of them "shape" up to become their habit helpers.

In the first draft of this book I titled this section, "The Mind Shapers." Later I decided it wasn't true to my human equation because the mind is only one of the two inputs to behavior. Moreover, in an Orwellian society that America is becoming, while not missing any opportunities to shape the minds of the masses, it is their behavior that our "Big Brother(s)" needs to control because it is the consequences of that behavior on a massive scale that really matters to them. Supportive and docile behavior has very different consequences from rebellious behavior for an oppressive state.

I quote Orwell and Skinner because they knew a thing or two about shaping behavior. It doesn't matter that black box psychologist Skinner believed behavior can be shaped just by shaping the person's situations and that Orwell added the mind into the mix. Nor does it matter that one wrote a famous novel describing a utopian society while the other wrote an even more famous novel describing a dystopian society; if they were alive today I am certain both would rail against our dystopian society.

While some of the other habit helpers could also be considered behavior shapers, that is not, I believe, how they would characterize themselves. The behavior shapers I have in mind here are think tanks, shams, religion, education, the news media, the PR industry, and the entertainment industry. The differences among some of them can be gossamer thin.

Think Tanks

A certain "tank" of people with IQs over 130 is the "Mensa Society," not a "think tank" in common parlance. My guess from reading what comes out of the common think tanks is that their IQ's are, well, more common. Think tanks also go by other names such as policy institute and research institute. Most are not-for-profit, non-governmental organizations (NGOs). Some are front groups for the corpocracy. The think thanks I have in mind here are ones with an ideological and activist agenda.

"Two of Washington's most bellicose think tanks," wrote staff writer Will Sommer of the Washington City Paper, are the American Security Council Foundation and the Center for Security Policy. Sommer tells the amusing story about these two feuding over who has the trademark right to the slogan, "Peace Through Strength." [14]

Those two think tanks are just two of over 120 groups that Right Web, an outfit that "tracks militarist efforts to influence foreign policy" has on its list. [15] A tiny sample of the others includes the American Enterprise Institute, the Bipartisan Policy Center, the Claremont Institute, the Committee on the Present Danger, the Emergency Committee for Israel, the Ethics and Public Policy Center, the Foundation for Defense of Democracies, Freedom House, the Heritage Foundation, the National Endowment for Democracy, the New American Century, and the NGO Monitor. The motto of one of them is "fighting terrorism and promoting freedom" but it could surely speak for the rest. The American flag so tightly wrapped around them and American money flooding them have choked off and drowned real think tanking.

Of particular relevance here are think tanks that think about warring and spying and probably little else, and that would probably include those two most bellicose think tanks in Washington, DC. Interestingly, they did not surface in an analysis that identified seven think tanks deep not in unbiased, critical thought but in defense contractor pockets making a self-serving pitch for launching a military attack on Syria. [16]

I ought to include here people who are what I call free-wheeling zealots who may not belong to any think tank. These zealots are mostly ideologues who come in two indistinguishable shades, the neoconservatives and the neoliberals. As Philip Giraldi, a former CIA counter-terrorism specialist and military intelligence officer noted about the candidates for the 2008 presidential election, "Neoconservatives and neoliberals are really quite similar---The American public---will still get war either way." [17] Let that sink in Mr. and Mrs. America.

Shams

They are a motley lot but they all share at least one thing in common. They pretend to be what they are not, so they are not unlike some of the think tanks. There are two groups of shams, compromised non-profit organizations (NGOs) and front groups. As with all the other behavior shapers, these two groups are not mutually exclusive.

Most NGOs are tax exempt. So right out of the starter's gate they are saddled with a quid pro quo. I call it "hush money." [18] Favors are exchanged. The regime loses some revenue by shelling out the hush money but gets to temper the activist NGOs that could be troublesome if not indebted to the regime. Some of these NGOs also accept foundation and corporate money, which hushes them further. NGOs compromised by the corpocracy have been called the "non-profit industrial complex." [19]

Front groups camouflage their real purpose, euphemize it, or obfuscate it. Most front groups are backed by corporate interests and promote those interests. The war and spy industries don't really need to depend on front groups. [20] There is no pretense about their lobbying groups. An exception may be the group, "Fix the Debt." If you read its material you realize not much is said about fixing the defense loaded national debt. The reason is that the group is tied to over 40 defense contractors such as Boeing and Northrop Grumman. [21]

Religion

> *As he died to make men holy,*
> *let us die to make men free.*
> *While God is marching on.*
> ---Julia Ward Howe's Battle Hymn of the
> Republic

> *We are bringing God to the soldiers and*
> *the soldiers to God.*
> > ---Army chaplains' motto
> *Stay on the battlefield nd kill Muslims for*
> *Christ*
> ---Evangelical chaplains' advice

Julia Ward Howe, the daughter of a wealthy New York City banker, was touring Union army camps along with her husband, a member of President Lincoln's Military Sanitary Commission, and a minister. She was so inspired that she wrote, at a safe distance from any battlefield the Battle Hymn of the Republic. [22] Forever thereafter it has become one of the spiritual rallying songs for war patriots.

Army chaplains are about as close as any God-fearing humans can get to the battlefield save those doing the fighting and/or dying from it. "What an opportunity to be with those young soldiers now as a mentor and as an encourager to give them spiritual motivation," exclaimed the Army Chaplain who was being interviewed and who recited that quoted motto. [23] Catch the pathetic irony in that motto?

Some Army chaplains who are evangelical Christians have reportedly advised soldiers seeking mental health counseling from the stress of battle to return to it and target the Muslims for Christian capital punishment and sending them I suppose to the Devil instead of to God. [24]

Religion and its sacred scriptures full of violent passages has provided the spiritual motivation and the spiritual rationalizations for wars and violence ever since deities were invented and battles fought. America was just one of the newest lands where deadly beliefs in the supernatural could be practiced. Remember the Puritans? There was nothing pure about their savage intolerance of alien beliefs (e.g., the 17th century burning to death of 400 some "Godless" Pequot Indians, and the Salem witch trials in which 20 mostly women were executed for practicing what the God-fearing townspeople believed was witchcraft).

Since religion is the art of "seeing what is believed," not of "believing what is seen," it is perfectly understandable that from the moment many millennia ago creatures walked upright and started explaining natural "mysteries" there would sprout and grow to this day countless religions that tolerate if not promote wars and violence. Religious fundamentalism in general and the Christian right in particular, for example, have tended to be outright war hawks. [25]

But no matter what their faith, how many religious leaders in America can we expect to tell their flocks to protest America's warring and spying habits? Since a majority of Americans approve of drone strikes, for example, my guess is that a majority of religious leaders do also either because of their convictions or their moral cowardice.

As I was writing this book I responded to the doorbell ring from four nicely dressed, polite proselytizers from an evangelical religious organization with eight million members. I asked what its official position was on the regime's deadly drone strikes. They told me it was neutral. I then said that if Christ were alive today we can be fairly certain he would not have been neutral. Eight million neutral members! If only they and the other 100 some million spiritual believers would clamor in unison for peace at the fence of the White House and foot of Capitol Hill they would be heard and heeded.

Before moving on I want to emphasize that I am not against religion per se, just dogmatic, hurtful religious beliefs, believers, and practices, especially those that condone if not also promote war instead of peace. While there are passages of unspeakable violence and cruelty in sacred scriptures there are also peace making passages.

Education

Religion and education are much alike. Both receive government funds. Both are a source of employment. Both cross over sometimes into the other's territory. Both start with young formative minds. Both fill those minds with doctrines, leaving little room left for critical reasoning to question those doctrines, including learning how to discover and distinguish real knowledge from beliefs. Both help sustain America's warring and spying habits.

The roots of American education were grounded in two necessities. One was the need for the Industrial Revolution to depend on, as the wit and social critic, H.L. Mencken put it, "a standardized citizenry." [26] The other was the need to help get America ready for WWI, and so the American Council on Education was hurriedly formed to ensure a supply of trained military personnel. [27]

Since WWI and Mr. Mencken's time American education, whether the public or private version, has had to endure countless critics. And the critics are often right but not always for the right reasons. The evidence for what this American education produces is all around us and is often described in very unflattering terms; the uneducated American, the functionally illiterate American, the dumbed-down American, the moronic or idiot American.

But this is not the place to go into a discourse on the dysfunctional condition of American education. That has already been done by many authoritative critics. [28] This, instead, is the place to illustrate briefly some of the ways in which the regime directly and indirectly influences American education and through it young minds by making and implementing educational policies; by infiltrating early school years; by actually teaching warring and spying; by constantly putting on displays of jingoistic patriotism; and by using public high schools as recruiting stations.

By Affecting Educational Policy

All three levels of government; federal, state, and local, shape America's youth not through socially responsible and quality teaching but through administrative policy making and implementation. I will give you four examples, one at the State level and three at the Federal level.

At the State level the Alaska State Board of Education requires that one military representative be appointed as an advisory member of the board. At the Federal level The Morrill Act of 1862 establishing land grant colleges mandated the teaching of military tactics. Then there was the American Council on Education already mentioned.

Later, during the Eisenhower administration, concerned that that the military was not getting the qualified people it needed led to the passage of the National Defense Education Act. Mind you, it was not called the National Education Act. Our federal government down through the years in effect has been telling the taxpayers that some of their money for "education" goes first to meet the needs of its habits.

By Infiltrating the Classroom

Of all the humanities' subjects the teaching of American history is the most vulnerable to "militarization." As the saying goes, history belongs to the victors. Their wars are the facts to which self-serving reasons are given and conclusions drawn. I can't imagine my 13 litmus tests for wars (see Appendix A) would ever be on the agenda of many if any American schools. Teaching about war in America's classrooms tells American youth "This is what America does to defend freedom," not, "This is what America does in pursuit of its 'manifest destiny' to rule and exploit the world."

Let's consider, for example, how the deadly and divisive Civil War and Vietnam War get treated in the classroom. They don't get ignored because that would be a glaring omission. But they aren't exactly "taught" either. They are propagandized and rationalized.

In a feature article for the Washington Post on the occasion of the sesquicentennial of the Civil War, reporter Nick Anderson tells about how fourth graders in a school in Virginia, a state that had been embroiled in the war, built and floated models of two war ships to reenact the naval Battle of Hampton Roads. [29] Reenactments are a perfect tool of the establishment. They are entertaining and they teach children how to think and act militarily. Children are taught the obligatory rationale that abolition of slavery was the war's reason, with no mention of Lincoln's racism and imperialistic reasons for keeping the nation intact for future expansion. [30]

Now let's move forward from the end of that war to the Vietnam War, one of the most senseless and shameful wars America ever waged. Few high school students apparently are told how joyous the Vietnam people were over regaining their independence once America left humiliated in defeat or that a string of five American presidents and their administrations lied about the reason for that war, starting with President Truman when America first supported France's attempt to retain colonial rule of Vietnam and then took over when France failed. America's corporate/militaristic state had no intention of letting Vietnam rule itself. Although there's passing mention of the revealing "Pentagon Papers" in high school textbooks, few if any apparently delve into those papers or quote Daniel Ellsberg's conclusion that, "It wasn't that we were on the wrong side; we were the wrong side." [31]

Even if a classroom textbook were more rather than less objective and comprehensive about America's history, teachers are not independent agents and must be careful what they teach from the textbook and beyond it. Teachers who question or criticize America's warring and spying risk losing their jobs and some have. [32] It is thus hardly surprising that most social studies teachers in America spend scant time on controversial issues such as America's wars and discourage students from talking or writing about them. [33] Administrators who fire teachers for what they teach have the backing of the U.S. Supreme Court, which has never ruled against America's warring and spying, and believes it's perfectly constitutional to muzzle teachers. [34]

By Actually Teaching Warring and Spying

Not for an instant would I think that that fourth grade teacher meant to actually teach her pupils elementary naval battle maneuvers to be remembered and perfected as they continue their education. That opportunity comes later in a variety of ways, and the war/spy complex doesn't miss any of them. One of the most blatant examples that I know about is the Air Force's "CyberPatriot" program to teach middle and high school students with the aim of recruiting them later for careers in cyber security. [35] I would call that "grooming future spies in the skies."

Then there's the case of Chicago's public school system, reportedly "the most militarized in the country, boasting five military academies, nearly three dozen smaller Junior Reserve Officer Training Corps programs within existing high schools, and numerous middle school Junior ROTC programs---nearly all located in low-income, minority neighborhoods." [36] Arne Duncan, the person apparently most responsible for this militarized education in the Windy city was its CEO of public schools who later became President Obama's Secretary of Education. This probably means that as Chicago goes so does the nation.

What could be considered as sort of an enlarged, walk-in classroom are museums that imbue impressionable young minds with the "patriotic" spirit of war. For example, "The Price of Freedom: Americans at War" is an ongoing exhibit at the National Museum of American History in the nation's capital. David Swanson, author of numerous anti-war books says "The exhibit is an extravaganza of lies and deceptions," but then adds that "---overwhelmingly

147

the lying is done in this exhibit by omission. Bad past excuses for wars are ignored, the death and destruction is ignored or falsely reduced." [37] Then there are museums just for the Marine Corps, the Navy, the Coast Guard, the Army (under construction) and for the spy arm (the International Spy Museum) of our government that help the young and old learn to accept its twin addictions.

Moving up to adulthood the war and spy agencies take total charge and turn the education of young adults into targeted (s)kill training. What do schools like Kansas State University, the University of North Dakota and the private Embry-Riddle Aeronautical University have in common?

They offer "feet-on-the-ground" four-year degrees in drone piloting. One student graduated with a 4.0 GPA and landed a job "as a flight operator for a military contractor in Afghanistan." [38] Within our own borders the market is also growing for trained operators of drones for domestic surveillance, and it won't be long before the FAA, concerned about drone crashes over our heads, drops its ban so that eager, militarized, money squandering local police departments will no longer be confined to practicing with their new drone planes over warehouse parking lots. [39]

Don't laugh. Conceivably there will be some day MDs (Masters of Drones) and PhDs (Doctors of Drones).

Moving on, there's the Reserve Officer Training Corps (ROTC) program on state college campuses. The Vietnam War protests torpedoed compulsory ROTC (I was forced to take two years' worth in the early 50's) and several of its programs were ejected from their campuses. In recent years however it has reappeared at some universities.

There are the online Military University, the U.S. Army War College (nothing subtle about its agenda) and the familiar military academies like West Point. Not to be left out, spies have their own "university," the probably less familiar National Intelligence University that offers undergraduate and graduate degrees in the basic and advanced science of intelligence-where the "BS" and "MS" degrees could stand for "basic and masterful spying respectively."

Finally, in Fort Bennington, Georgia there's what used to be called "The School of Assassins" (pejorative nickname for "The School of Americas") because Latin American dictators and their thugs were trained there in the fine arts of torturing and killing dissidents who threatened the dictator's rule and America's parasitic corporations in their countries. The school's sordid reputation eventually became so embarrassing that the school was given a new name, the Western Hemisphere Institute for Security Cooperation. [40]

> *Military men are just dumb, stupid animals*
> *to be used as pawns in foreign policy.*
> ---Henry Kissinger

The "statesman" actually made that un-statesman-like comment. [41] While I am anti-war I do not believe "military men are just dumb, stupid animals." They just got a militarized education that taught them to follow orders traceable to people like the "statesman." And as a matter of conjecture, couldn't America's statesmen and stateswomen (only three of 68 U.S. Secretaries of State have been women) just as easily if not accurately be referred to as dumb, stupid members of the regime in power?

By Displays of Jingoistic Patriotism

Before textbooks are opened in children's classrooms across America the Pledge of Allegiance is most likely to be recited. In one of its more judicious reversals, the US Supreme Court changed its mind and ruled that public school children no longer could be compelled to recite the pledge, and added in the majority opinion that---"no official, high or petty, can prescribe what shall be orthodox in politics, nationalism, religion, or other matters of opinion or force citizens to confess by word or act their faith therein." [42] Try telling that, however, to young children anxious to conform and to void being bullied.

Outside the classroom are many other arranged opportunities for the expression of jingoistic patriotism, such as flag waving, honor guards, uniformed parading, and the like at school assemblies and sporting events. Recall my discussion of the "twisted meaning of loyalty." Bad loyalty is jingoistic patriotism, which is not earned but expected by a state that accepts nothing less from its public than fealty to the state. Bad loyalty depends on emotionalism. Bad loyalty is like Hitlerism. Good loyalty is unwavering support of a good cause, a good person, a good state. Good loyalty, like respect, is earned. Good loyalty is more a reasoned than an emotional response. A nation that instills bad loyalty in its youth in the service of ignoble ends is unworthy of any loyalty. Good loyalty is to a real democracy. Bad loyalty is to a corpocracy masquerading as a democracy with flags, anthems and pledges.

By Captive Recruiting

Ever since conscription was ended to avoid protests on the scale of the Vietnam War protests the military has had difficulty in getting new soldiers, especially in war time, which is standard USA Time. To take up the slack waivers have been given by the Army and Marines to felons, allowing them to join---now they can loot in foreign lands. [43] Additionally, and of more pertinence here is that Congress has allowed military recruiters to scour available personal information about 11th and 12th graders and to go into public high schools hunting potential recruits instead of relying only on walk-ins to downtown recruiting offices. "It was overwhelming. To get to lunch in my high school, you had to pass recruiters,---I thought the recruiters had too much information about me." a college student told a reporter, who added that "Before an Army recruiter even picks up the phone to call a prospect---the soldier may know more about the kid's habits than do his own parents." [44]

> *Hello, Billy?*
> *This is Corporal Armor*
> *Your grades and martial arts*
> *hobby are really impressive*
> *You could go far in the Army*
> ---The author

Mainstream Media

> *Scare the Hell out of the American people.*
> ---Senator Arthur Vandenberg

Harry Truman went from being a haberdasher to ordering the dropping of Big Boy and Fat Boy on Japan. Then, from his "black box" swelling with hubris, arrogance and what have you, he told America and the world about his new "Truman Doctrine." Its purpose said Senator Vandenberg was to "scare the Hell out of the American

151

people." [45] It did just that and, since it followed the dropping of his nuclear bombs, also scared the Hell out of the Russians, thus provoking the Cold War and profiting the war and spy industries on both sides.

Had Truman stuck to haberdashery subsequent history might have possibly been a little less bloody. Anyway, the point here is that Truman did not walk around the country telling millions of Americans face to face about his bellicose doctrine. He used the media and it played and trumpeted his speech over and over for all it was worth.

The mainstream, corporatized media has never stopped being a dependable mouthpiece for U.S. militarism and imperialism. Listen, for instance, to what Philip Giraldi, a former CIA counter-terrorism specialist and military intelligence officer had to say about the media's reporting of the Bush administration's buildup to the invasion of Iraq: "Many journalists and former government officials were surely aware that the intelligence was being cooked. I was at the CIA at that time and many working level officers were walking the halls shaking their heads and wondering what was going on, so it wasn't as if no one knew. But the mainstream media refused to touch the alternative story in any serious way." [46]

The mainstream media refused because it was, and still is, a partner with whatever regime is in power. Paradoxically, it was a mainstream newspaper that occasionally rebels, The New York Times, and on one of those occasions it successfully sued the Department of Defense to gain access to some 8,000 pages showing how the agency's senior officials plotted and played the American people for fools by massaging and manipulating the news Americans got about the build up to and then the conduct of the Iraq War.

152

And was the news ever massaged and manipulated! Joseph Goebbels, Hitler's propaganda chief would have been envious. I always knew we were being bamboozled by the Bush administration through the partnering media but I didn't know the behind-the-scene details of all the plotting and theatrics involved until only recently when I read an article by the Pulitzer Prize winning journalist, David Barstow, in The Times. [47] It is a very long article, but such a must-read one that I am going to summarize it here.

How the Pentagon and the Media Sold the Iraqi War

> *What you see and hear is not what you get.*
> ---Dave Barstow

Mr. Barstow must have done some exhaustive reading of those 8,000 pages before writing his article. It depicts how the Pentagon's top officials with the White House closely monitoring the process and progress masterfully marshaled and primed retired military brass to be the administration's mouthpiece. They were called "military analysts" to give them the sheen of authority and authoritativeness. Some were paid according to how many convincing appearances they made on the major networks (Fox, ABC, NBC, CNN, MSNBC) watched by millions of viewers (some analysts also wrote propaganda articles in newspapers). A few of the brass were willing to admit they had been submitted to brainwashing and were in turn doing the same to the public, but the networks were mostly mum or circumspect when asked about the analysts' roles, their ties to the defense industry, and their messages.

I am going to continue summarizing his article that describes how the mainstream media misled the public about the regime preparing to invade Iraq and then how the mainstream media misled the public about the war's progress. [48]

Selling the Public on Invading Iraq

The administration's propaganda campaign seems to have begun in response to bad publicity about treatment of imprisoned "terrorists" at Guantanamo. With DoD and its Secretary taking the lead, a team of military analysts was assembled and flown there while being fully briefed in the air by DoD people on what to say. After the staged visit, the analysts, being good ventriloquists "went on TV and radio, ---criticizing calls to close the facility and asserting that all detainees were treated humanely." Tell that to the detainees.

During detailed planning for a possible Iraq invasion, Pentagon and White House officials, worried about possible public objection since there was no clear connection between Iraq and the 9/11 terrorist attacks, realized it would be far more believable if not they but retired military brass, "most of them decorated war heroes" and portrayed as highly authoritative analysts "in the news media, [but] not of the news media" were to sell the public on an invasion. Eventually the Pentagon recruited over 75 retired officers, some already affiliated with the major networks. Secretary Donald Rumsfeld cleared all of the analysts while the White House screened initial lists and suggested new recruits.

Besides being primed for their mission the recruits were preened by the Pentagon in the process to leave nothing to chance. They were taken by "uniformed escorts to Mr. Rumsfeld's private conference room, the best government china laid out, the embossed name cards, the blizzard of PowerPoints, the solicitations of advice and counsel, the

154

appeals to duty and country, the warm thank you notes from the secretary himself."

The campaign went into high gear as the time for the invasion approached. One of the recurring themes parroted by the recruits was the imminent threat of Americans being rained on by "weapons of massive destruction" despite the fact there wasn't a shred of evidence to buttress the warning. The public was also assured that "an invasion would be a relatively quick and inexpensive 'war of liberation.'"

Misleading the Public on a Failing War

The hype about a quick and easy invasion had to be turned quickly into hyped reassurances as the war started failing, and reports of mounting US fatalities were surfacing. A Pentagon strategy memorandum urged that it was time "'to re-energize surrogates and message-force multipliers,' starting with the military analysts," and taking them on a tour of Iraq. Despite the fact that the American viceroy in Iraq had privately expressed his gloomy assessment to President Bush, the analysts were given a carefully scripted, positive briefing before their visits to carefully selected and controlled sites in Iraq such as brief visits to "a few refurbished government buildings."

Returning to America and the networks the analysts gave glowing reports of progress to the public but a few analysts were very candid in their private remarks. A retired general, for instance, upon returning from the Iraqi tour joked about how "artificial" the briefings had been, while another commented that he had seen "immediately in 2003 that things were going south." There were also some analysts who, even before the war started, doubted the justification for the invasion, but were careful not to express their doubts on the air.

In April 2006, Secretary Rumsfeld's propaganda campaign was badly punctured when several former generals not among the scripted analysts went public criticizing his "wartime performance" and some "called for his resignation." Faced with this personal crisis he had to ramp up the show again and call upon his analysts to go public defending him. He called them in to his office to discuss damage control. Very soon afterwards the reliable "analysts hit the airwaves" and dutifully repeated "many of the Pentagon's talking points," downplayed the criticisms, and talked about "the next milestone in Iraq, the formation of a new government."

This finishes my summary of Barstow's article. The Bush administration is history. Iraq, a devastated nation in turmoil, faces an uncertain future and likely will be a tender box for years to come. In the meantime, the Obama administration, like the one before it, is helped by the media in justifying U.S. drone strikes and military forays into yet more countries, including renewed bombings in Iraq and in keeping quiet about the resolution in Congress that would give the "green light" for Obama to go to war with Russia. [49]. If cooler heads don't prevail that green light could jump start Armageddon (see Chapter 8).

The PR Industry

PR and BS The similarity can be deadly
---The author

The media provide the medium. The PR people prepare the message. Scratch an assistant secretary for public affairs or any other political appointee presiding over public relations for the war and spy agencies and you are likely to find underneath a former executive in the public relations industry, the two-sided business of promoting the positives and accentuating the negatives dressed up as positives.

Take the case of Torie Clarke, a former PR executive turned assistant secretary of defense for public affairs in the Pentagon. Mr. Barstow wrote about how "even before Sept. 11, she built a system within the Pentagon to recruit "key influentials" — movers and shakers from all walks who with the proper ministrations might be counted on to generate support for Mr. Rumsfeld's priorities." [50]

All or most of the war and spy agencies have public relations or public affairs offices. They are a smaller bureaucracy within a larger bureaucracy. Billions of dollars are being spent by taxpayers so that the bureaucrats and their contractors can turn around and spin the tax payers.

Some of the PR is just traditional advertising with brand names and brand pushing. Can you match the following military service slogans that appear on the airwaves, newsprints and internet that target young men and women between the ages of 16 and 21? "Be All You Can Be." "Get an Edge on Life." "It's Not just a job. It's an Adventure!" "You and the ___" "Full Speed Ahead." "The Few, The Proud, The ___." "We're Looking For a Few Good Men." " Aim High. Be Part of the Action." If you can't match the last one with the Coast Guard neither could 97% of the targeted youth a DoD contractor surveyed. If, on the other hand, you matched the first slogan with the Army so too did 91% of the surveyed youth (maybe the Coast Guard PR people need to be replaced). [51] If you are a sports fan you probably matched most of them correctly for they appear on televised major league baseball, professional football, professional basketball, and professional motor racing.

But according to investigative journalist Joseph Trento and his two co-author apprentices war and spy PR (the latter provide damage control spin for publicity-shy spies) has turned the corner into the new age of "strategic communications" aimed at the American people, with juicy contracts let to private contractors. The three authors end their long investigative report concluding that "There are only two institutions large enough to provide "checks" on the military and intelligence communities: Congress and the media. Congress chooses not to do its job. The media no longer can." [52]

The Entertainment Industry

> *Hollywood*
> *Not Real War and Spy*
> *But Reel War and Spy*
> ---The Author

Early on in graduate school my wife and I went to see the movie, Exodus, shortly after it had been released, about the "founding" (or stealing depending on point of view) of a new land for a new nation. I was mesmerized (as were many movie reviewers) but soon forgot about it as I was neck deep in my studies. Years later, my head up from the textbooks and exams, I realized I had been scammed by a slick Hollywood production aimed to garner public sympathy and continued support for Eretz Israel. [53] It succeeded. Most Americans through the years haven't

158

objected to being fleeced billions of dollars by their government in its fortifying and defending a country that could in a flick of distemper ignite WWIII.

Hollywood has had a "reel" interest in Washington's wars and foreign policy affairs ever since it made training and propaganda films for President Woodrow Wilson's administration in support of WWI. [54] Hollywood was far more active and sophisticated in how it cinematically promoted WWII. [55] Today, it is glamorizing and propagandizing American torture and militarism in movies like Zero Dark Thirty, Black Hawk Dawn, and Argo (a movie "glorifying the CIA" and handed the best picture award by Michelle Obama, First Lady), to mention just a "few major recent productions showing how today's movie industry promotes US foreign policy." [56] A later propaganda piece from Hollywood is "World War Z," which Jeffrey Goldberg, a columnist for Bloomberg View, hailed as "the most pro-Israel movie ever made." [57]

There's a cozy quid pro quo between Hollywood and the military and national security complex. Hollywood submits its war glorifying movie scripts to the complex for review and gets access to dazzling military equipment to use for props in profitable movies. The complex, in turn, gets dazzling PR aimed at movie goers.

During the Roman Empire some 50 thousand people would throng to the Coliseum to watch gladiators fight to death and Christians being thrown to the lions. The American Empire is a tad bit more civilized with its multibillion dollar business of amateur and professional sports in which there are relatively few deaths but lots of injuries. Millions of Americans are fans of one or more sports. It is a golden opportunity for the military with its bloated budget to showcase itself by sponsoring events and to attend them in full dress regalia. I recall the spectacle of two NCAA Division One basketball teams playing an exhibition on an aircraft carrier. I'm a moderate fan of that sport, but not when it's played on aircraft carriers.

The Toy Industry

From toy pistols for small hands to sophisticated, interactive WiFi war games for pre-teens. The toy industry has carved out its own niche so I will treat it separately rather than include it as part of the entertainment industry.

Our younger daughter vowed that her young boys would not be allowed to play with guns or war games. The vow melted. Now older, but still pre-teen they have advanced in their simulated killings to sophisticated, interactive WiFi war games. And I must confess that their grandfather, yours truly, gave them as presents in their younger days a few "blaster" guns. While I doubt very much that they will someday become real warriors or spies, I worry that they are possibly being shaped into passive bystanders, a massive collection of human beings we will come to shortly.

The toy industry is obviously sensitive as its trade association issued the following statement in 2013 on the subject of "toy guns and violence:" "The Toy Industry Association (TIA) and its members are proud of the important, life-shaping role that toys, games and play have in the development and growth of children." [58] Unwittingly or not they were acknowledging the "life-shaping role" of their industry's products, precisely the point I want to make here, that violent toys and games, especially the highly popular video games put the players,

160

at least certain kinds of "black box" players at risk for behaving antisocially in real life.

Do scientific studies back up this point? Science that is even well done on social issues hedges its conclusions because there are so many factors in children's lives that can confound the results and conclusions. Nevertheless, the findings from a multitude of studies on violent video games does seem to corroborate the intuitively obvious; namely, that even games that are clearly make-believe have the undesirable effect of increasing aggressive behavior, and desensitizing the perception of violence not only among young children but among older age groups as well. [59]

To finish this section on the behavior shapers I want to add this personal note. I don't consider myself a brilliant person. I had to work hard to get my advanced education and then some professional achievements here and there afterwards. But since I was a gullible viewer of Exodus I can well imagine how the typical American is like putty to be molded by any or all of the behavior shapers accommodating a warring and spying regime.

The Gun Industry
Real Toys for Big Boys

Were it not for the campaign donations and intensive lobbying by the handgun industry and its powerful lobbyist, the National Rifle Association, that have burdened America with indiscriminate gun buying by the public, I would treat the industry as an adjunct to the entertainment industry, although with apologies to wildlife like deer not entertained in being shot to death. But the gun industry and the 2nd Amendment misinterpretations and the Supreme Court's misruling are what they are and so we have in America a population that almost equals the population of citizen's guns, virtually no gun control, and far more gun related violence and death compared to other "advanced" countries. That this is so is not a coincidence with the fact that the regime is gun happy.

Why is it not a coincidence? A possible explanation comes to mind. America from the beginning has fought rather than negotiated international disputes and in that beginning guns (muskets) were available. "In guns we trust" eventually became officialdom's unofficial motto. Americans have become accustomed and indifferent to American guns at home and away, giving war mongering politicians' carte blanch to create enemies and then have their military ("let others do it)" fight them. For most Americans bloodshed becomes out of sight and out of mind unless one is in a school, theater, or mall with a gun firing psychopath. Otherwise, where our guns are used seems to go on deaf ears.

That the U.K., a warring country most of its history has one of the lowest rates of gun deaths, may seem to refute that explanation until we know that private guns are banned in that country and that it is no longer the militaristic empire it once was. [60] A good legal test of the explanation will probably never be forthcoming, nor will the banning of private and public guns in America. The ban would incite a civil revolution.

Science

Big Boy and Fat Boy
Created by Mad Scientists
Ordered Dropped by a Mad President

Hurtling Two Cities into Destruction,
Death, and History
---The Author

Science discovers. Science plus the war/spy habits destroy. To say that the nuclear discovery also led to nuclear medicine, while apparently true, salves the conscience. Also true is that science mixed with peace would have led to nuclear medicine (the same goes for the rationalizations that other wonders such as the Internet, GPS, and the computer mouse are byproducts of military and intelligence research).

Science research and development (R&D) are a yearly multi-billion dollar enterprise, almost all of it funded by the federal government. My guess is that the biggest chunk of that money is spent on R&D for war and spy gadgetry (trying to pin down figures is like going blindfolded on a "Treasury" hunt).

Some of the subjects researched and gadgets developed sound right out of George Orwell and science fiction. [61] Here is a partial list of gadgets (a complete list would only be known by a few unknown people) either in operation or on the drawing board:

> Air and underground drones
>
> Cocktails to wake up drowsy soldiers
>
> Dust particles that are miniature sensors
> Exoskeleton suits for herculean feats
> Explosive sensing bees
> Fire sensing cockroaches
> Flying, tiny bird sized cameras
> Genetically modified soldiers
> Ghost radio
> Implanted microchips

Insect-sized drones to inspect caves for
terrorists
Monkeys' thought-controlled movements
Radar rats
Robotic soldiers toting machine guns
Sea lion sentries
Secret gadgets too secret to know

Billions of dollars go into thinking up, tinkering with and making those oddities. Just imagine if the money and minds represented by that list were spent instead on peacetime R & D for new sources of energy, cures for the incurable, and the like. But no, we live in a mad, mad world and Frankenstein America is at the center of it.

Take a look again at all of the defense and intelligence contractors listed in Appendix D. Most of those outfits are beehives of R & D activity I'm sure. One of them, for instance, is Battelle Memorial Institute. It is a private nonprofit applied science and technology development company. It is exempt from taxation because it is a "charitable" trust organized as a nonprofit corporation. One of its three business divisions doesn't sound charitable at all: National Security Chemical, Biological, Radiological, Nuclear and Explosive technologies, Aerospace, Maritime and Ground Systems, Environmental Systems and Energetic Systems. That is a foul mouth full.

And did you notice that The Johns Hopkins University was also on the list? Clicking on its website will get you eventually to the Applied Physics Laboratory of that university. It is a not-for-profit, university-affiliated research center employing 4,500 people and is primarily a defense contractor for the Department of Defense, NASA, and other government agencies.

164

The "hard" sciences (e.g., chemistry, physics, etc.) aren't the only ones cashing in on the R&D cash cow. So do some if not all of the "soft" or social sciences such as psychology and anthropology.

War has always been a boon for psychology. Psychologists, for instance, developed the testing of military personnel for WWI. [62] In WWII Skinner used his specialty, experimental psychology, to teach pigeons how to guide bombs, but the military decided to capitalize on new, less cumbersome radar equipment and dropped the bombs without the pigeons' help. Some psychologists apparently were quick to take advantage of the Bush administration's "war on terror" initiative and reportedly became involved in helping to test different interrogation and torture techniques, and possible evidence and allegations of collaborations between the American Psychological Association and the CIA have been surfacing. [63]

A field of social science I almost considered choosing instead of psychology, and a field that at first blush might seem irrelevant is that of anthropology. Yet its roots in warring and spying are older than those of psychology. Early American anthropologists collaborated with the military in its forays against Native Americans, and a president of the American Anthropological Association was censured by it in 1919 after he criticized scholars who served as spies during World War I. [64]

The social sciences need to read and react to what Ralph Nader wrote recently about them. From crusading against unsafe autos and the corpocracy in general and an unfortunately but predictably failed run at the White House he has now turned his critical eye to the social sciences; has found them essentially socially useless; and then has provided "--- a brief list of contemporary needs that could benefit from academic specialists [in the social sciences] who are concerned and knowledgeable about our country's shortcomings and could know how to get things moving." Noting that "A society that has more justice needs less charity [both a trite and a profound observation), he suggests that the social sciences could find ways to "reach and motivate enlightened billionaires" who have told him (assuming they were being honest) that "they have little idea of how to effectively put their money to work for justice, so they continue giving to charities." [65] I should point out a less charitable interpretation of what these billionaires' motivations might really be; namely, they get tax deductions from charities, and charities are not about to upset the wealth and power pyramid.

Hard science is called "pure" science, the "R" without the "D." All science in the service of the war and spy monster is "impure" science.

Foreign Enemies

In order to bring a nation to support the burdens of maintaining great military establishments, it is necessaryto create an emotional state akin to war psychology. There must be the portrayal of external menace.

---John Foster Dulles

Dulles was Ike's Secretary of State, the very same Ike that supported the Vietnam War as a way to prevent "a tremendous loss of prestige" shortly before he wrote his disingenuous and hypocritical valedictory address warning the nation of the "military industrial complex," one that he presided over, allowed it to grow, and used it covertly to get puppet regimes installed here and there. [66]

But more to the point here is that the hardliner Dulles was merely stating the obvious from the perspective of any imperialistic regime. How many American politicians and political appointees do you know or remember who ever told the American people "we must create enemies to justify our military budget" or "we want to control the resources of Country X," instead of disguising the truth by saying "Country X is a threat to American security."

Recall my saying that making sure America has enemies is a most potent badvantage." If there is no enemy de jour (as if that has ever happened) the regime in power trumps up an imaginary one or provokes a potential friend into becoming a foe.

The Cold War, for instance, was a mutually manufactured convenience for both the American and Russian regimes. They were allies, albeit perhaps strained ones in WWII, but each for its own aggrandizement soaked their own public treasuries in gearing up for and rattling each other during the Cold War. But it was neither Reagan's militancy nor the Cold War strain on the Soviet Union's economy that dissolved the confederation of the Eastern bloc countries. Rather, it was the result of internal political policies by Gorbachev and his successor Yeltsin and the disaffection and political ambitions of a few members of the confederation that spelled its end.

One of Gorbachev's confidants reportedly said as the Soviet Union was dissolving, "We are going to do a terrible thing to you in the West: We are going to deprive you of your enemy." [67] He obviously underestimated the determination of America's regimes to create new enemies to whet the insatiable appetite of the world's military superpower.

America's regimes think nothing of turning potential friends into enemies. During the Vietnam War, for instance, a Viet Cong soldier reportedly asked an American soldier, "Why do you fight us, we admire America?" [68] I doubt if the American soldier knew the real two-fold answer; LBJ wanted to look tough so as not to lose the presidency to Barry Goldwater, and secondly, his regime wanted a foothold in that region, not to prevent its "dominoes from falling" but its resources from escaping corporate America's clutches.

Sociologist Charles Derber contends that "---today's regime "can survive only by practicing a foreign policy of bad faith that [he calls] 'marry-your-enemy.'" [69] I would put it a bit differently; "any American regime gives birth to enemies," which reflects the correct direction of cause and effect. America's enemies are the effect of America's actions, not the cause of them.

"At last the American government has found," says author and antiwar activist Jim McCluskey, "the perfect formula for war without end: Invade and bomb Middle East states. This creates jihadists which must be got rid of. So bomb the jihadists. This creates more jihadists who must also be bombed and so on. The military/industrial complex is in business in perpetuity." [70] My only quibble with Mr. McCluskey is that our government found that "perfect formula" much, much, earlier than he thinks.

Bystanders: The Silent Americans

They are everywhere, millions and millions of them. If I were to name the largest category of silent Americans it would be religious denominations with millions of members that eschew any official condemnations of military operations that slaughter countless human beings. These denominations, of course, are not to be confused with the war hawks of the radical Christian right and the "messianic hard-right rabbis---[who]incite mass murder." [71]

In general bystanders on war and spy matters include people who may oppose those matters but is basically silent and inactive about them. The millions of Americans who say when polled that they disapprove of the regime's drone strike killings, for example, but do not actively protest against them are bystanders. The Vietnam War protestors, on the other hand, were clearly not bystanders.

There are many reasons why silent Americans are silent about the real signs of warring and spying, about the killing of innocent foreign children, for instance, by drone strikes. When we get to a certain particular reason I will tell you that it was my reason for being "carefully-silent" for many years.

The Signs Aren't Seen for What They Really Are

They aren't seen by people for whom believing is seeing. Believing that America is threatened by enemies, for example, is seeing that the threat exists and warrants warring and spying. The nationalistic belief in America's superiority and manifest destiny is seeing that America is always justified in its international relations.

They aren't seen by people who have never been taught how to think critically and analytically, so they fail to understand how terrorists are created by America's warring and spying, not the other way around.

They aren't seen because they are "an inconvenient truth" denied by people who would otherwise feel threatened or helpless if they didn't deny seeing the signs or rationalize them away.

They aren't seen by people who compare America favorably to the world's most totalitarian nations.

They aren't seen by people who have become accustomed to them, taking them for granted as just the normal workings of America's government.

They aren't seen by people who haven't directly felt their effects; who haven't had loved ones injured, killed, or interrogated.

They aren't seen by people with a particular upbringing. Children reared in a very dominating setting, for example, come to know life as being a choice between dominating and being dominated. [72]

They aren't seen by people for whom the signs are ambiguous or their nature hidden or falsified. Does spying on us, for example, protect our freedom or rob us of it and our privacy? Were there really, for example, the WMDs?

The Signs Are Seen For What They Really Are, But

The people seeing them just don't care. Self-centeredness is morally irresponsible and to the extreme is pathological psychologically and socially. When enough of these people live in the same nation it becomes a sociopathic society. [73]

The people seeing them feel helpless up against the mightiest regime the world has ever seen.

The people seeing them are fatalistic about their future, believing that whatever happens will happen.

The people seeing them are worn down, preoccupied by the daily grind of living, and just trying to make ends meet.

The people seeing them don't want to jeopardize their comfortable stations in life. I was this kind of bystander during my entire career. I detested the U.S. involvement in Vietnam before the U.S. escalated its involvement into a full-fledged war. My family and friends knew my views but I did not go out and shout them on the streets. This book is sort of my atonement for having been a bystander and a coward.

Jay Janson, an archival research, peoples' historian activist, musician and writer, has another name for bystanders. He calls them "accessories after the fact" since they meet that term's legal definition that is codified in U.S. law. [74]

Is there any wonder that the Habit Helpers outnumber by millions the addicts in the warring and spying complex? Is it any wonder that America's two chronic and costly habits persist?

Before ending this chapter I want to mention a slightly different take on "How Americans are Seduced by War." [75] I am referring to the subtitle of a book by Andrew Bacevich, professor of international relations at Boston University. The "new American militarism," he says is fueled by several factors: warriors-in-chiefs that emphasize even more than their predecessors the use of military force; the military profession itself, the emergence of the neoconservative ideologues; Hollywood; hawkish Christian conservatives; narrow minded scientists; and overemphasis on the Middle East. Several of those factors you will notice are among those analyzed in this chapter.

Endnotes

1. Lendman, S. Banker Occupation: Waging Financial War on Humanity. Clarity Press, Inc., 2012.

2. Ibid.

3. Center for Progressive Economics. Monetary Quotes from the Famous.

4. www.brainyquotes.com Note: While this is a widely cited quote the Archives and Library staff of the Henry Ford Benson Ford Research Center could not verify its authenticity.

5. Brown, EH. Web of Debt: The Shocking Truth about Our Money System and How We Can Break Free. Third Millennium Press, 2011. 5. www.wikiquotes.org

6. Nace, T. Gangs of America: The Rise of Corporate Power and the Disabling of Democracy. San Francisco: Berrett-Koehler, 2003.

7. Brumback, GB. The Devil's Marriage: Break Up the Corpocracy or Leave Democracy in the Lurch. Author House, 2011, 151-152.

8. Rivero, M. All Wars are Bankers' Wars! What Really Happened. January 14, 2013 Radio Show. www.whatreallyhappened.com

9. Rothbard, MN. Wall Street, Banks, and American Foreign Policy. www.lewrockwell.com

10. Rothbard, MN. Ibid..See also, Eley, T. & Grey, B. Obama's Wall Street Cabinet. World Socialist Web Site, www.wsws.org, April 6, 2009.

11. The Revelation: New World Order Quotes. David Rockefeller, founder of the Trilateral Commission, in an address to a meeting of The Trilateral Commission, in June, 1991. www.theforbiddenknowledge.com/quotes/, undated.

12. Orwell, G. 1984. Harcourt, Brace and Company, 1949.

13. Skinner, BF. Walden Two. Macmillan, 1948; Orwell. Ibid.

14. Sommer, W. No Peace for Hawkish Think Tanks Over Reagan Slogan. Washington City Paper, September 14, 2012.

15. Right Web. Tracking Militarists' Efforts to Influence U.S. Foreign Policy. http://rightweb.irc-online.org.

16. Public Accountability Initiative. Conflicts of Interest in the Syria Debate. October 11, 2013.

17. Giraldi, P. Neolibs and Neocons, United and Interchangeable. AntiWar.com. August 14, 2007.

18. Brumback, GB. Tyranny's Hush Money. OpEdNews, September 28; The Greanville Post, September 29, 2013.

19. INCITE. The Revolution Will Not Be Funded: Beyond the Non-Profit Industrial Complex. South End Press, 2009.

20. Megalli, M. & Friedman, A. Masks of Deception: Corporate Front Groups in America. Washington, DC: Essential Information, December, 1991.

21. Galbraith, R.& Connor, K. Operation Fiscal Bluff : How the "Fix the Debt" Budget Lobby is Protecting Billions in Defense Contracts for its Corporate Backers. Public Accountability Initiative, December, 2012.

22. Tubb, BR. Civil War Music: The Battle Hymn of the Republic. The Civil War Trust, undated.

23. Abernethy, B. Army Chaplain Boot Camp. Religion and Ethics Newsweekly, April 4, 2008.

24. Rodda, C. Chaplains and Religion Substituted for Professional Mental Health Care in the Military. Huff Post Religion, May 25, 2011.

25. See, e.g., these articles by Frank Schaeffer, a prolific book and New York Times best-selling author, film director, screen writer, and public speaker: Fundamentalist Religion Will Destroy The World. OpEdNews.com, July 3, 2011; How Christian Fundamentalism Helped Empower the Top 1% to Exploit the 99%. OpEdNews.com, October 16, 2011; and, We Need Ethical Evolution, Not More Destructive Fundamentalist "Certainty." HuffPost Religion, November 14, 2013.

26. Mencken quote: Think Exist.com

27. The American Council on Education. http://www.acenet.edu

28. This alphabetized list of sources about the condition of American education and its "pupils" hardly scratches the surface but includes a few that have been informative for me: Gatto, JT. The Underground History of American Education: A Schoolteacher's Intimate Investigation into the Problem of Modern Schooling. NY: The Oxford Village Press Oxford, 2000; Hedges, C. The Perversion of Scholarship. Truthdig.com, July 30, 2012; Kohn, A. The 500-Pound Gorilla: The Corporate Role in the High-stakes Testing Obsession & Other Methods of Turning Education into a Business. Phi Delta Kappan, October, 2002; Lendman, S. A Nation of Morons. OpEdNews, April 26, 2012; Livergood, ND. The Destruction of American Education And What We Must Do About It. OpEdNews, August 31, 2012; McGettigan, T. A Bungling Fox in the Henhouse: The Corporatization of Higher Education. OpEdNews, December 7, 2011; Payne, M. Corporatism's Plan for the Dumbing Down of America. OpEdNews, May 17, 2012; Wolchover, N. People Aren't Smart Enough for Democracy to Flourish, Scientists Say. Live Science,

February 28, 2012; Pierce, CP. Idiot America: How Stupidity Became a Virtue in the Land of the Free. NY: Doubleday, 2009; Simon, S. U.S. Spends Big on Education, but Results Lag Many Nations: OECD. Reuters, June24, 2013; and Washburn, J. University, Inc.: The Corporate Corruption of American Higher Education. Basic Books, 2005.

29. Anderson, N. Teaching the Civil War, 150 years later. The Washington Post, April 10, 2011.

30. Zinn, H. A People's History of the United States. Harper Perennial, 2005, 188; 198. See also discussion of the Civil War in Appendix A.

31. Bigelow, B. Camouflaging the Vietnam War: How Textbooks Continue to Keep the Pentagon Papers a Secret. HuffPostPolitics, June 21, 2013.

32. See, e.g., Hathaway, W.T. From Cheerleader to Enemy of the State. Dissident Voice, February 18, 2013; and Zimmerman, J. What's Not Being Taught about the Iraq War. Salon, March, 2013.

33. Zimmerman, J. Ibid..

34. Wikipedia. Pledge of Allegiance.

35. Mead, C. Military Recruiters Have Gone Too Far: The Pentagon is Using Video Games to Infiltrate Middle Schools. Time.com, September, 17, 2013.

36. Kroll, A. The Duncan Doctrine: The Military-Corporate Legacy of the New Secretary of Education. TomDispatch.com, January 18, 2009.

37. Swanson, D. Teach the Children War. OpEdNews,com, March 20, 2013.

38. Raftery, I. Anticipating Domestic Boom, Colleges Rev up Drone Piloting Programs. NBC News, January 29, 2013.

39. Raftery, I. Ibid.

40. Wikipedia. The Schools of America.

41. Bernstein, C. & Woodward, B. The Final Days. Simon & Schuster; Reissue edition, 2005, 194.

42. CNN. Army, Marines Give Waivers to More Felons CNN.com/US, April 21, 2008.

43. Alvarez, L. Army Giving More Waivers in Recruiting. The New York Times Online, February 14, 2007.

44. Goodman, D. A Few Good Kids? How the No Child Left Behind Act Allowed Military Recruiters to Collect Info on Millions of Unsuspecting Teens. Mother Jones, September/October 2009.

45. Skidmore, D. Reversing Course: Carter's Foreign Policy, Domestic Politics, and the Failure of Reform. Vanderbilt University Press, 1996, 17.

46. Giraldi, P. Failed by the Fourth Estate. OpEdNews,com, April 4, 2013.

47. Barstow, D. Behind TV Analysts, Pentagon's Hidden Hand. The New York Times, April 20, 2008.

48. Mr. Barstow is not responsible for my summary. Its quotes are from his article.

49. Global Research. Fighting the Battle Against Mainstream Media Disinformation. Global Research, December 7, 2014.

50. Barstow, D. Ibid.

51. Hintze, W. Recognition of Military Advertising Slogans among American Youth. Google Books, 1999.

52. Trento, J., Weltemeyer, C.& Gaskill, B. The Selling of The Pentagon 2013. DC Bureau, September 30, 2013.

53. See, e.g., Victor, JM. Politics, Cinema, and the Middle East: Reconsidering Exodus. New Society, Harvard College, January 29, 2008.

54. Levesque, J. Screen Propaganda, Hollywood and the CIA. Global Research, February 28, 2013.

55. See, e.g., Denby, D. Hollywood at War. The New Yorker, March 17, 2014, 69-73.

56. See, e.g., Levesque, J. Op. Cit.; and Scheer, R. Oscar 2013: Hollywood's CIA Celebration. OpEdNews.com, February 26, 2013.

57. Bloomfield, D. Deconstructing The 'Most Pro-Israel' Zombie Movie Ever Made. The Jewish Daily Forward, July 19, 2013.

58. TIA. Toy Industry Association (TIA) Statement on Toy Guns and Violence. October 29, 2013.

59. See, e.g., Anderson, CA. Violent Video Games: Myths, Facts, and Unanswered Questions. Psychological Science Agenda, American Psychological Association, October 2003.

60. See, e.g., Leber, J. The Scientific Case for Outlawing Guns. MIT Technology Review, February 7, 2013; and Rogers, H. Gun Control. An International Comparison. Independent Voter Network, July 25, 2012.

61. See, e.g., Bier, J. Defense Dept. to Spend Up to $4 Billion for R&D on Combating Weapons of Mass Destruction. The Weekly Standard, December 16, 2013; Locker, R. Pentagon Boosting its Push for Underwater Drones. USA Today, March 13, 2014; and Rossi, M. What Every American Should Know About Who's Really Running the World: The people, Corporations, and Organizations that Control Our Future. Plume, 2005. 246-251.

62. Koppes, L (2007). "History of Industrial Organizational Psychology in North America." Encyclopedia of Industrial and Organizational Psychology. Ed. Steven G. Rogelberg. Vol. 1. Thousand Oaks, CA: Sage Reference, 2007. 312-317. Gale Virtual Reference Library. Web. 5 Mar. 2011.

63. Eidelson, R. Dr. Frankenstein and the APA's Decade of Monstrosities. OpEdNews.com, August 28, 2012. See also: Eidelson, R. & Bond, T. New Evidence Links CIA to APA's "War on Terror" Ethics. OpEdNews, October 14, 2014; and, Risen, J. Pay Any Price: Greed, Power, and

Endless War. Houghton Mifflin Harcourt, 2014; and and Gray, G. Weaponizing Psychology. Counterpunch, Decembe 24, 2014.

64. See, e.g., Price, D. Weaponizing Anthropology: Social Science in the Service of the Militarized State. AK Press; Reprint edition, 2011; and Jaschik, S. If CIA Calls, Should Anthropology Answer? Inside Higher Ed, September 1, 2006.

65. Nader, R. Thanksgiving for Social Scientists: Wish It Were. Dissident Voice, November 27, 2014.

66. The quotation of Mr. Dulles is from Parenti, M. Messianic Nationalism: The American Perspective, 262 in Harrison, T.W. and Drakulic, S. (Eds). Against Orthodoxy: Studies in Nationalism. UBC Press, 2011; my reference to President Eisenhower's farewell address can be found in Greenberg, D. Beware the Military-Industrial Complex. Slate Magazine, January 4, 2011.

67. Oberg, J. Brisbane: A show of Western Weakness. Transnational Foundation for Peace & Future Research, November 18, 2014.

68. Brumback, GB. A Deadly Monster: Part 1: An Overview of the Military-National Security, Industrial, Political Triumvirate. Dissident Voice, December 11, 2012.

69. Derber, C. Regime Change Begins at Home: Freeing America from Corporate Rule, 2004, 100.

70. McCluskey, J. Endless War for Perpetual Peace. Dissident Voice, October 8, 2014.

71. Lendman, S. Profile of Imperial Lawlessness. OpEdNews, February 26, 2013.

72. Eisler, R. The Real Wealth of Nations: Creating a Caring Economics. Berrett-Koehler, 2007.

73. See, e.g., Derber, C. Sociopathic Society: A People's Sociology of the United States. Paradigm Publishers, 2013; and Kall, R. Chomsky Talks about Psychopaths and Sociopaths. OpEdNews, February 15, 2014.

74. Janson, J. Michael! Call For US Crimes Prosecution End Our Being Accessories After the Fact! OpEdNews, December 24, 2012.

75. Bacevich, AJ. The New Militarism: How Americans are Seduced by War. Oxford University Press, 2005; this book is reviewed by James Webb in his article, What is it Good For? How the U.S. Military Went from Defense to Offense. The American Scholar, Spring 2005, Vol. 74 Issue 2, 135-139.

CHAPTER 7
BREAKING THE HABITS

This chapter is sort of a "How-to-manual." It is not an AA 12-Step program. It's an AA 7-Step program, where AA stands for Alter America. Let me give you a little backgrounder.

In the Afterword of The Devil's Marriage I envisioned a model of a rebuilt America. I called the model "Alter America." [1] Its characteristics would be remarkably different from the real America in six ways.

First there would be a democracy and no corpocracy.

Second, America would be a peace making and internationally law abiding nation, not the warring and spying scofflaw it has always been.

Third, America would be an egalitarian or partnership society, not a male dominated society that it has always been. Remember, it was the Founding "Fathers." America has always had male warriors-in-chiefs, male dominated legislatures and judiciaries, and almost totally imperialistic male CEOs and financiers. Males on top throughout a society produces a "dominator society," says Riane Eisler, a best-selling author, who has studied this prevailing mode of social and economic structures and cultures throughout the history of the world. The dominator society, she says, "has four core elements: rigid top-down control; intense abuse and violence" manifested (my pun intended) in "child and wife beating; chronic warfare;" "the rigid ranking" of men over women; and a culture of stories, beliefs, and the like that "justify domination and violence as inevitable, even moral."[2] In contrast, Eisler calls the ideal model the "partnership" society. Few societies, one of them being Finland she says, come close to this model, that of a democratic, egalitarian, and non-violent family and social structure.

Fourth, America's economic system would depend on the production of socially beneficial products and services and not on using other peoples' money to make money. Every American inhabitant would be guaranteed an adequate standard of living (as stipulated by Article 25 of the 1948 United Nation's Declaration of Universal Human Rights) and the opportunity to a fulfilling and meaningful life as envisioned by the late Abraham Maslow in his hierarchical theory of human needs and motivations. [3]

Fifth, there would be no more government handouts to corporations, and as a result corporations would have to organize much differently and be run much differently or fail. [4]

Sixth, America would be a just society that respects citizens' rights and holds them, government, and all business and finance organizations accountable for how they discharge their responsibilities.

There you have my vision of an Alter America. Envisioning it was easy. Achieving it is a totally different matter and just may be an impossible dream, as impossible to realize as one or more of the five scenarios described in the last chapter may be possible if America doesn't reverse course.

In the Devil's Marriage I presented a comprehensive plan that included over 400 initiatives for achieving political, judicial, economic, and social reforms that would be necessary for ending the corpocracy and creating an Alter America. The initiatives for breaking America's two habits were just a small piece of the overall strategy.

I am not going to repeat here that whole plan to create Alter America. Instead, I am going to concentrate exclusively and freshly on how the two habits can be broken. Breaking them would not end the corpocracy completely and create an Alter America, but would achieve the miraculous outcome of an America at peace with the world, which is undoubtedly the most important characteristic of Alter America, undoubtedly the most important outcome for the world, and undoubtedly the most difficult reform goal.

In the Devil's Marriage chapter on ending the warring habit I proposed an all-out blitz, "Waging War on War," that called for launching these initiatives:

Establish the Citizens' Assembly of Peace
Establish the Department of Peace Keeping
and National Security
Establish a Peace Keeping and National
Security Council
Nationalize and reorient the defense
industry
Join the International Criminal Court
Create a dual draft
End the propagandizing of the military and
militarism
Determine the lost opportunity costs of
warfare welfare
Impeach/prosecute officials who commit the
U.S. to war on false pretenses

Permanently ban and prosecute defense
contractors who defraud the government
Publish a detailed "name and shame" annual
warfare welfare report
Stop budget overruns in military spending
Stop emergency and off-the-book defense
budgeting and funding
Include supplemental funding and nuclear
weapons funding in military budget
Require open and competitive bidding on
all contract bids
Purge the GNP index of defense costs
Prevent war profiteering
Stop the manufacture and purchase of
useless weapons
Stop the sale anywhere abroad of arms
from U.S. manufacturers
Eliminate privatization of the military
Forbid military recruiting at public schools
and colleges
Eliminate college ROTC programs Suspend
the U.S. Peace Corps while the U.S. is at
war

I am not going to pour over this anti-war list again that
admittedly looks like a wish list. Instead, what follows
next is a more targeted 7-Step AA strategy for breaking
the two habits.

The Alter America Plan

Step 1. Establish a Citizens' Assembly for Peace

There are hundreds of small to large peace and antiwar non-governmental organizations (NGO). They obviously have not succeeded in stemming the incessant rush to war. But that outcome is beyond their grasp given their relatively miniscule budgets (a very few multimillion dollar ones) and, more significantly, their disunity and thus no overall strategic plan and coordinated effort to end America's endless warring.

Here is a list of some of the more prominent organizations:

American Friends Service Committee
afsc.org
ANSWER: Anti-War Committee
answercoalition.org
Center for Nonviolent Solutions
nonviolentsolution.org
Center on Conscience & War
centeronconscience.org
Center for Peace and Justice georgefox.edu
Christian Peacemaker Teams cpt.org
Code Pink: Women for Peace
codepinkalert.org
Creating a Culture of Peace
creatingacultureofpeace.org
Education for Peace in Iraq Center epc-usa.org
Episcopal Peace Fellowship
.epfnational.org
Fellowship of Reconciliation forusa.org

Friends Committee on National Legislation
fcnl.org
Global Network Against Weapons &
Nuclear Power in Space space4peace.org
Granny Peace Brigade.
grannypeacebrigade.org
International Fellowship of Reconciliation
ifor.org
International Women's Peace Service:
Nonviolence In Action iwps.info/en/
Iraq Veterans Against The War ivaw.org
Just Foreign Policy justforeignpolicy.org
National Network to End the War Against
Iraq endthewar.org
National War Tax Resistance Coordinating
Committee nwtrcc.org
NGO Committee on Disarmament, Peace
and Security disarm.igc.org
Nonviolent Peaceforce
nonviolentpeaceforce.org
Nonviolence International
nonviolenceinternational.net
Nuclear Age Peace Foundation napf.org
Peace Action peace-action.org
Peace Alliance thepeacealliance.org
Peace Brigades International
peacebrigades.org
Peace Jam peacejam.org
The Peace Resource Center prscd.org
Physicians for Social Responsibility psr.org
Religions for Peace religionsforpeace.org
Resource Centre of Non-Violence rcnv.org
United National Antiwar Coalition
nationalpeaceconference.org
Veterans for Peace veteransforpeace.org
Vietnam Veterans Against War vvaw.org

Voices for Creative Nonviolence vcnv.org
Voices of Conscience
voicesofconscience.com
War Resisters' International wri-irg.org
War Resisters League warresisters.org
Win Without War WinWithoutWarUS.org
Women's International League for Peace
and Freedom wilpfus.org
World Beyond War worldbeyondwar.org
The World Can't Wait worldcantwait.net

These organizations collectively have the potential, however, to make significant strides toward a more peaceful nation and world if they could somehow be persuaded to collaborate and form the nucleus of a Citizens' Assembly for Peace, building it possibly from the ground up with assemblies in the States and geographical regions. Unifying the disparate peace and antiwar organizations is so obvious an approach to take that I am not alone in proposing it. Lawrence S. Wittner, for instance, who is a professor of history and once a member of Peace Action's board, has argued for "a powerful national peace organization, with a mass membership."[5] Then there's Gareth Porter, peace activist, book author and winner of the prestigious Gelhorn Prize for journalism, makes the same point. "On the larger plane of what peace activists can do, I think that the first order of business is to get organized." [6]

All right, Professor Wittner and Mr. Porter, why not a Citizens' Assembly for Peace? Let's assume it happens after several conferences of peace activists were held around the country and the consensus was to establish the Assembly. Let's assume it is championed by a number of prominent and respected leaders (e.g., former U.S. Attorney General Ramsey Clarke, former Congressman

Dennis Kucinich, Congresswoman Barbara Lee, and crusader Ralph Nader).

For the sake of some brevity, the rest of this section is full of implicit "let's assumes."

The Assembly has received multi-million dollar grants from one or more of the many antiwar foundations; sizable donations from the wealthier of the peace and anti-war NGOs; has hired leadership and staff; has created a steering council, has organized the network into a set of strategic alliances; and has developed a plan to carry out several major strategic initiatives (as already noted a more modest and perhaps more realistic beginning would be to start from the ground up with the establishment of Assemblies in local communities).

The alliances would group together NGOs with expertise in work required by the strategic initiatives. There might be, for example, a media alliance to publicize the Assembly and keep the public informed; an outreach alliance to build the Peace Coalition (explained shortly); a political alliance to deal with the political obstacles to change; a legal and regulatory reform alliance to deal with legal and regulatory obstacles to change; a think tank alliance to research issues; and an industrial issues alliance to deal with the war and intelligence industries.

The Assembly has authorized these strategic initiatives: publicize the Assembly's launching; start the Peace Coalition; change the politics of warring and spying; and help the military and intelligence industries to gear their work toward peace time products and services. These initiatives are the remaining steps of the program

Step 2. Publicize the Assembly's Launching

America and the world would need to know about the "birth" of the Assembly. Let's start with the warring and spying politicians in Washington, which amounts to almost all of them.

2a. Tell the Politicians

The Assembly would send certified, return receipt, personally addressed letters asking the politicians in Washington to sign a pledge to stop America's warring and spying pronto. They would be told that that the Assembly and the Peace Coalition are gaining strength and will return later with a "tsunami" of pressure if the pledges aren't signed.

The nation's warrior-in-chief would also be asked to go before the United Nations and give an address promising a peaceful America. The address would be like the one shown in Exhibit A. It is the same as the one I sent President Obama suggesting he give it as part of his first inaugural address. I never got a response. No real surprise there! He was already trapped by his black box and badvantages. Had he delivered this address and did what I said he would do America would have become a peaceful nation.

Exhibit A
Proposed UN Address by America's President

*As members of the international community neither we
nor you should continue along the hurtful paths of our
past. The world is smaller, making its problems bigger.
When any one of us oversteps the boundaries of helpful*

188

international behavior our hurtful footprints are felt world-wide. It is in all of our interests and for generations yet born to enter a new dawn of international friendship, cooperation, and peace.

To that end I am inviting you to join with me in creating a Global Goodwill Network under the auspices of the UN to seek ways to make our smaller world a more peaceful and habitable one for all its inhabitants. I am going to ensure that America abides by the rule of law and will sign and get ratified America's membership on the International Criminal Court. A world in which countries trade fairly among themselves will be a world more at peace than at war, so I intend to ensure that America's business transactions with the rest of the world will be fair ones and that exploitative globalization by multinational corporations headquartered in the U.S. ceases.

I intend with the help of Congress to rethink and alter our approach to economic, foreign, and military policy and will accelerate withdrawal of our combat forces and military bases on foreign soil. I will insist that in return for continued U.S. support of both sides there absolutely must be a two-state solution to the Israeli-Palestinian conflict.

I will shore up our obligations and support for a reformed and reinvigorated UN that encourages localized markets, not globalized ones. I will also propose creation of a new UN entity, The Councils of the Continents, with each having the primary responsibility for restoring goodwill in their own territories. For those who join us we shall establish cooperative partnerships. For those who choose not to do so, we shall keep inviting you."

As we have seen both chambers of Congress are loaded with committees and subcommittees setting military budgets, overseeing military spending, making and unmaking laws and regulations favorable and unfavorable to the war-national security industry, and influencing the Departments of War/Defense, Homeland Security, and Energy to hand out large contracts in the right places. Members of those committees need to be among the prime targets for pressurized reform. Lesser but still prime targets need to be all the rest of Congress, starting with those Congressional districts ranking the highest in "dollar value of total defense contracts" (in 2006 the top five were 1. Virginia's 8th district: $11.789 billion to 985 defense contractors; 2. Virginia's 10th district: $6.096 billion to 664 defense contractors; 3. California's 53rd district: $3.034 billion to 325 defense contractors; 4. Virginia's 11th district: $2.931 billion to 514 defense contractors; 5. Alabama's 1st district: $2.585 billion to 335 defense contractors). [7]

Ralph Nader has proposed a watchdog group in each of the more than 400 Congressional districts. [8] That is a great idea. I would simply add creation of a local chamber of democracy or a local Assembly for Peace in each of those districts having not only the responsibility of monitoring their representatives but also of pressuring them until the pressure becomes intolerable. These local groups also need to be pressuring war and intelligence contractors to start converting to peacetime work.

Letters would also be delivered to state legislators and governors asking for their support of the Assembly's objective. Politicians in states where war and intelligence contractors are located, which would mean most if not all states, would be told the contractors are also being contacted.

2b. Tell the Agency Heads

The heads of the war and intelligence agencies would get a manifesto telling them to get ready for peace and privacy and to give the president their full support if he decides to call a halt to warring and spying.

2c. Tell High Ranking, Retired Military and Intelligence Officers

Recently in Israel 106 retired, high level officers wrote a letter to the nation's prime minister urging him to "make peace." [9] Can you imagine, for example, many retired, high-level military and intelligence officers in the U.S. writing President Obama telling him to start making peace with our global neighbors?

It conceivably could happen. These officers have the opportunity to reflect on their careers and how gratifying they were or were not, say, in terms of the late psychologist Maslow's hierarchy of human needs and motivations that I mentioned earlier. As a psychologist myself I would have to think that there is some degree of regret and time to reflect on what they could do differently for America's future. A letter from the Assembly might nudge some of them to emulate the retired Israeli officers. Of course, neither Mr. Obama nor his successor might budge any more than did Prime Minister Netanyahu.

2d. Tell Corporate America

The CEOs and boards of directors not only of the war and intelligence contractors but throughout corporate America, including Wall Street and the mainstream media would be asked to pledge cooperation with the Assembly's objective. The war and spy contractors would be offered assistance in shifting to peacetime services and products.

2e. Tell America at Large

The media alliance would blitz the airwaves, the newsprint, and the highways (billboards) and public events (e.g., sports arenas). Since the mainstream media are captives of the corpocracy, equal time would have to be demanded. Besides announcing the Assembly, Americans would be asked to join the Peace Coalition that is being started.

The general public would also need to be blitzed with four blunt messages: 1. America's enemies are the result of, not the cause of America's endless warring and spying. 2. America could have friends instead of enemies if she ends her warring and spying. 3. Without your help America will not end her warring and spying. 4. America will eventually end if she doesn't end her warring and spying.

Step 3. Start the Peace Coalition

Any major reform initiative in America that calls for an overhaul of the regime's policies and practices is dead in the water without substantial political pressure from the general public. There have been very few major social reforms and no reforms in the military and intelligence area. America's political regimes throughout the years have cleverly controlled public dissent by tolerating it up to a point and by making small concessions they are willing to tolerate. [10] That is exactly why most NGOs are exempt from taxes and some receive government funding as well. Regimes, moreover, are quite content with the oppositions' mantra of reform through a "thousand cuts" as long as those cuts are never unified into one un-surmountable cut. Regimes also have no compunctions about assassinating prominent dissidents with huge followings. According to the conclusion of a prominent judicial tribunal, that is apparently what happened to the Rev. Dr. Martin Luther King, Jr. [11]

The Assembly would thus need to build a massive protest movement of millions of Americans and organize them into the Peace Coalition headed by some nationally prominent figure such as a Kucinich, a Lee, or a Nader and given a compelling slogan such as "linking arms against arms. The Coalition's purpose would be to provide political pressure behind each initiative. This pressure would need to be applied relentlessly on the regime. It must be made to understand that it is under a siege that won't let up, that a monumental civil, legal and nonviolent "war" is being waged on its warring and spying, and that any mollifications or compromises initiated by the regime would be unacceptable.

3a. Inventory Potential Habit Breakers

Habit breakers, as I've said, are people who might have a reason to join the Coalition. They are people who are opposed to or might be persuaded to oppose America's warring and spying and to join the Coalition. The Assembly needs to find out who those people are.

Even unlikely sources need to be considered. For example, there are the "behavior shapers" mentioned in the previous chapter. Surely some of them are capable of helping shape public opinion away from tolerating America's warring and spying.

The millions of individual members who donate to antiwar organizations and to all allied NGOs ought to be recruited. Surely a substantial number of them are not front groups and/or have not been compromised by the regime.

Another source for finding potential habit breakers would be those segments of the general public on the following list that conceivably are discontented with one of more aspects of the American experience, especially warring and spying:

Exhibit B

Potential Habit Breakers?

Aggrieved victims of injustice
Angry voters
Authors and journalists
Bloggers (there are numerous antiwar
blog sites)
Business and public servant exemplars
Consumer groups
Creative arts (the antithesis of warring
and spying)
Enlightened super wealthy
Front line volunteers (e.g. soup kitchens)
Grass roots movements
Individual social activists
Millennials
Occupy movement and its many groups
Organized religion (the positive elements
of it)
Party twin alternatives (i.e. not
Republicans or Democrats)

Peace and feminist groups (other than NGOs) Professional groups
Responsible corporate owners
Senior citizens with liberal or progressive orientation
Small businesses and their associations
Small farmers and their associations
Social entrepreneurs
Twitter People
Unions

In The Devil's Marriage I gave a detailed rationale for why I picked each segment while acknowledging that some would be very doubtful (e.g., religious organizations?). I will not repeat the rationales here except to say that I had not considered adding the "enlightened super wealthy" until I learned why Ralph Nader chose them. He explained that, "One percent of the citizenry diversely organized in congressional districts and reflecting the "public sentiment" can turn around, perhaps with the funding support of an enlightened billionaire or two, the Congress and the White House." [12] It's a grand idea, but the stumbling block I should think would not be finding one or two of those billionaires but in mobilizing and coordinating about 25 million American adults.

There is no doubt that well over 25 million Americans are disaffected for one reason or another with any ruling regime. Represented on the list, for example, are undoubtedly some or all of the 27 percent of polled Americans who disapprove of our warrior-in-chief's drone strikes and the 21 percent of polled Americans dissatisfied with their lack of freedom over their own lives. [13] Some 70 million Americans are represented in those two polls.

But the discontent goes even further. According to recent polls "74% of Americans agree the broken political system needs to be fixed first; 86% believe political leaders are more interested in protecting their power than in doing what's right for the American people; 83% believe the country is run by an alliance of incumbent politicians, media pundits, lobbyists, and other interests for their own gain; 79% believe that powerful interests from Wall Street banks to corporations, unions, and PACs use campaign and lobbying money to rig the system to serve themselves and that they loot the national treasury at the expense of every American." [14] Those are impressive statistics, but they are just statistics until the Assembly figures out how to get all of those bystanders organized and out onto the streets.

Another potential source is, or at least was in the late 1990s, a huge international movement that needs to be mentioned. It is/was the anti-globalization movement of "tens of thousands of well-organized militant protesters" of two of the prime drivers of globalization, the International Monetary Fund and the World Bank.[15] They may just be a sleeping giant if it can be revived/steered toward becoming a branch of a peace coalition of social activists.

Another potential source, one totally outside the U.S. might be antiwar groups in other countries, particularly since most people in the world oppose U.S. drone strikes. There are also a few countries that have not been bribed into submission by U.S. foreign aid, that may or may not be members of NATO, and that might be willing to face the umbrage of the U.S. government. One such country is the Marshall Islands, a tiny nation that was a guinea pig for dozens of U.S. nuclear tests during the Cold War. It has sued the U.S. and eight other nuclear powers in the

International Court of Justice in The Hague, Netherlands, and also has filed a federal lawsuit against the United States in San Francisco, naming President Barack Obama, the departments and secretaries of defense and energy and the National Nuclear Security Administration. [16]

3b. Building the Peace Coalition

Building the Peace Coalition will probably be more difficult than establishing the Assembly for Peace. To forestall any more massive war movements on the order of the one against the Vietnam War Congress abolished the draft. And no unified, large antiwar movement has evolved since then even with the advent of the IRAQ War and its aftermath. The reason why that is so journalist and author David Sirota contends is that countless partisan activists quieted themselves when Obama was elected and haven't been able to mobilize since even though the President has surely disappointed, even angered them. [17] So what we have instead are relatively small and isolated antiwar protests scattered here and there and happening now and then in America without any overall strategy to steer them.

Other protests and movements seem to have diverted attention away from the regime's warring and spying. The Popular Resistance.Org Daily Digest reports daily on the activities of various movements and movement building resources in America. There are, to name a few, movements protesting environmental degradation (e.g., climate change, fracking, pipelines, tar sands, etc., etc.), and movements protesting GMO labeling, income inequality, international corporate trade agreements, racial injustice, police brutality, etc., etc. Randall Amster, JD, PhD, Director of the Program on Justice and Peace at

Georgetown University, Executive Director of the Peace and Justice Studies Association, and author of many books, refers to much of the foregoing as "flash mob" and "pop up protests." [18]

The solution to the lack of any unified antiwar movement or any unified movement for that matter may be found in the very meaning of the term "coalition," a union of separate elements that have some commonality. The commonality in this case is their grievances against America's corpocracy on a variety of injustices and conditions of life and the environment.

Commonality is a critical concept grounded in both theory and reality. The theory is the theory of connectivity, which posits that everything in life is interconnected, and I do mean absolutely everything. While my human equation is not prepared to stretch quite that far, I am convinced by reality that there is tightly webbed connectivity throughout the corpocracy, including its warring and spying components. An example of a tight connection is that between the military budget and domestic decay. The more money spent on the military the less money available to spend on domestic repairs. Climate change is another example of connectivity; in this case between environmental degradation and the military's devouring and spoiling of natural resources. The implication is crystal clear. End war and other military operations and help protect the environment and climate at the same time.

The Assembly thus needs to find and tell the leaders of these various movements to "connect the dots" among themselves and to understand that their grievances and those of antiwar and peace advocates have systemic roots planted long ago by America's corpocracy; that America's many sadtistics stem in part from the lost opportunity to rebuild America due to profligate military and intelligence spending; that the corpocracy's existence depends on divided opposition to it; that, therefore, these leaders need to unite their movements into one giant coalition; and that if they promise to do so the Assembly will rename the Peace Coalition the Alter America Coalition.

To jump start the coalition the Assembly could consider sponsoring a contest with a significant prize for the best slogan or motto to give the new movement. Two that come to my mind are "End War, Not America," "Making Friends, Not Enemies," and "Alter America or We'll Alter You."

Step 4. Change the Politics of Warring and Spying

This initiative involves several tactics. They target politicians and their situations (recall the human equation). Some of the tactics are less aggressive than others. Some are short term and some are long term. I am more ambivalent about some of them and less so about the rest of them. I will also comment on three tactics that I am not at all ambivalent about in not recommending them.

The tactic already mentioned of seeking politicians' pledges and the UN address is the least aggressive of those to come since the politicians undoubtedly would be non-responsive or ask for a meeting with no intention of complying.

4a. Bombard the Politicians with Petitions.

Petitioning requires little effort and accomplishes little unless there is a mountain of signatures that politicians can't ignore and that forces an acknowledgment and either a rationalized justification for not honoring the petition, or, unlikely, a commitment to honor it. Browsing the Internet just for "petitions to stop U.S. drone strikes" turned up 35 pages of listings (as of July 2014). Clearly, antiwar petitions are yet to change the black boxes. These petitions are an example of those "1000 cuts" I mentioned, and they might as well be cuts from sheathed knives.

Nevertheless, I try not to dismiss requests I get in my e-mail inbox to sign antiwar petitions. For example, I signed one on August 27, 2014 sent to me by Just Foreign Policy. The petition was being directed toward President Obama and Congress to avoid another endless war in the Middle East. I added this comment to my signed petition: "President Obama, warring and spying are America's oldest professions. You are swimming in a river of history. Please change rivers." The metaphor, you will recall from the third chapter was his own metaphor.

All antiwar petition makers ought to be contacted by the Assembly and persuaded to consolidate their petitions into one grand petition with up to 500,000 signatures and giving the regime an ultimatum. Offering it a compromise ought to be verboten. Mice should never sit at a table with a devil cat.

4b. Hold Massive Rallies and Protests

Joining rallies and protests requires more effort and, depending on the nature of the protests, risks law enforcement and legal retaliation. The last noteworthy antiwar protest helped end the Vietnam War, but then, as already mentioned, the war makers got smart and eliminated the draft and began hiring their help and adding bombers with empty cockpits.

I am reminded of an e-mail from Debra Sweet, director of the NGO, The World Can't Wait, announcing a protest at Obama's second inauguration parade that would include displaying scaled replicas of "at least 6 drones---brought from around the country." [19] While I wished Ms Sweet's protest well, I didn't make the long travel to the rally.

Millions of Americans would probably be needed for rallies and protests held throughout America, on the doorsteps of Capitol Hill, the White House, governors' mansions and state capitols to stop the real drones from flying. Anything less than a massive turnout tends to be symbolic and sometimes even looks theatrical or recreational. The biggest and most recent turnout seems to have been a rally in September 2014 of some 400 thousand climate control activists in New York City.

Note, by the way, that I am not including boycotts, a time-honored form of protest. Who other than Uncle Sam and the militarized police shop at the war and spy stores?

4c. Impeach and/or Prosecute and Convict the Criminals!

This tactic really ratchets up the aggressiveness notch. As we saw in the second chapter, warring and spying violate numerous domestic and international laws. That automatically makes the war and spy gang criminals and requires that they be held accountable "before the final judgment day" for their actions, although posthumous convictions need to be added after convictions of the warm bodied ones are made. Nixon, for example, ought to be tried from the grave for several criminal offenses, including his treasonous action of notifying the Viet Cong that they should wait and sign a more favorable peace treaty once he won the election over Hubert Humphrey.

Here again are some of the laws the war and spy people-the people with no sense of moral, legal or social responsibility-violate: First, Fourth, Fifth, Sixth, and Eight Amendments; Foreign Intelligence Surveillance Act (FISA); Geneva Convention's Article 3; Rome Statute (Article 7) of the International Criminal Court; UN Charter's Articles 2, 5, 33, and 51; U.S. Constitution Articles 1 and 3; and Whistleblower protection laws. These undesirables get by with their lawlessness because they are shielded from accountability, which is absolutely essential if a civilized society is to exist.

But how do you impeach and/or prosecute and convict them when they are also the law maker, the prosecutor, and the judge (over the history of the U.S. a spate of politicians have been convicted for minor felonies)? And they also refuse to join the International Criminal Court. They aren't stupid criminals, after all.

There are two forms of this tactic, symbolic and actual. While the Assembly would not discourage the first, the second would be the one the Assembly pursues with vigor. Let's consider impeachment first. Congress alone has the Constitutional authority to impeach a U.S. president, but that political body won't vote for impeachment on the grounds of warring and spying. The two branches see eye to eye on that issue. Yes, there was a Congressional hearing in 2008 in which a few prominent Democrats clamored for impeachment of Bush. But then Congress went back to its craven business as usual, with dulcet, political careerist Nancy Pelosi reportedly saying (probably sweetly) that "impeachment is off the table." [20]Congress isn't being spineless on the matter. They are protecting themselves as much as the president. They know that the war and spy industries butter their bread.

So until Congress can be put in a public pressure cooker, the Assembly needs to resuscitate the impeachment movement of local jurisdictions. During the Bush-Cheney reign of terror there were reportedly around 40 town councils in Vermont that had voted to have this pair impeached or arrested if not impeached. [21]

While these local tactics are basically symbolic, they are less so than verdicts by unofficial tribunals since the duo would think twice before visiting those towns. The duo needs to be made persona non-gratis wherever they go. Some Republican members of Congress have considered impeaching President Obama on grounds that are still unfocused. But Rep. Bob Goodlatte (R-Va.), chairman of the House Judiciary Committee reportedly was not interested, noting that "The Constitution is very clear as to what constitutes grounds for impeachment of the President of the United States. He has not committed the kind of criminal acts that call for that." [22] Representative Goodlatte, I have a good mind to send you a copy of this book with the paragraph five paragraphs above this one underlined. Are violations of those laws not high crimes?

As difficult as it may be to impeach public officials for their war crimes, the issue is not a dead one. The Assembly's litigation alliance needs to research all possible courses of action toward impeachment that should be considered. One source of information that is available, for example, is the "National Impeachment Resource Center" that was established by some prominent individuals who are very knowledgeable on matters of war and peace. [23]

Turning to prosecution and conviction of the war and spy gang, their virtual immunity is why so far any efforts to prosecute and convict them has been done mostly symbolically by having informal courts of justice handing down verdicts that carry no legal weight but do tell international war criminals and other associated scofflaws what august bodies of critics think about them and their conduct. The Russell Tribunal on international war criminals responsible for the Vietnam War is a famous example, and it has since spawned three successive Russell Tribunals on alleged war criminals and crimes against the people of Chile, Iraq, and Palestine. [24] Another example is the unanimous "conviction" of George W. Bush and five of his key aides in absentia of torture and war crimes by a tribunal held in Kuala Lumpur, Malaysia. [25]

The Assembly's litigation group needs to leave no stone unturned in finding and/or devising ways to proceed to nail the criminals through impeachment and/or prosecution and conviction. Some of its work has already been done for it by the Bush War Crimes Prosecution Conference convened in Andover, Massachusetts in 2008 by the prominent law school dean, Lawrence Velvel. [26] The conferees made 20 recommendations for actions that would sooner or later lead to prosecution of Georg W. Bush for his war crimes, but they apply equally well to any members of the war and spy gang.

The recommendations included such actions as prosecuting high level criminals for murder under state law; pursuing mandamus proceedings to force local prosecutors to act; holding a march of many thousands of

American lawyers on the Department of Justice to highlight lawyers' belief that crimes were committed and must be punished; seeking prosecutions of high level war criminals before foreign courts or before international tribunals such as the International Criminal Court; creating a truth and reconciliation commission; and impeaching, even after the culprits leave office.

There is another approach sometimes mentioned for holding war and spy criminals accountable that I call a form of "grass roots justice." This tactic calls for "ordinary" citizens to arrest war criminals, but the circumstances and conditions for doing so seem absolutely prohibitive and I know of no instances of them ever happening. The judiciary's immediate response to such an arrest would undoubtedly be that the citizen has no standing in court, but what if the citizen was a relative or spouse of a soldier killed on the battlefield?

Step 5. Reform the Political Party System

Step 5 is a longer term tactic and should not get in the way of the other steps. Politicians can't be separated from the political party system that they, the judiciary and corporate America control. The dominant, twin political parties, Democrat and Republican, have their bitter differences but they both are wedded to corporate America and addicted to the two habits.

Reforming the political system would be neither easy nor quick to say the least. But if the Assembly has the resources its political alliance of NGOs should consider one or more long term tactics aimed at such a reform. These tactics include creating or revitalizing a habit-free party; taking money out of politics; taking the voter out of politics, adopting a form of deliberative democracy; and pursuing federal ballot initiatives.

5a. Create or Revitalize a Habit-Free Political Party

In her book, Grand Illusion: The Myth of Voter Choice in a Two Party Tyranny, Theresa Amato, former campaign manager for Ralph Nader and founder of the NGO, Citizen Advocacy Center, says that unless one has been running a political race outside the two primary parties, "it is impossible to imagine the injustices of the two-party-tilted electoral process." [27] Third parties, not unlike thwarted eligible voters, run into all sorts of legal and other hurdles.

Nevertheless, third parties don't give up for trying. In the history of U.S. politics there have been some 800 third parties in all. Nearly 20 have nominated presidential candidates in recent times. Officially establishing a third party seems no more difficult than getting a driver's license and there's no quiz to take. What's nearly impossible is to get third party candidates elected because of the Constitutional roadblock to alternative voting procedures (such as, e.g., ranking votes received by all of the candidates) imposed by the Electoral College requirement of the Constitution. Removing the roadblock through a Constitutional Amendment would be next to impossible.

Two parties that embrace various positions against the corpocracy and for more direct participation by the citizenry in legislation and other political matters are the Progressive Party and the Populist Party. Of the two, the first seems to be the more active and robust. The Assembly's political alliance could decide whether to pursue their agenda within the context of the two major

206

parties or to promote one or the other of these two independent parties and along the way to try and get Ms Amato's proposed federal reforms implemented.

5b. Take Money Out of Politics

Habits are expensive. Money, time and energy must be spent to keep them going. America's war and spy habits are the most expensive habits the world has ever known and for which American taxpayers have ever had to empty half their pockets since the military budget alone consumes "half of every tax dollar." [28]

Take the money away and the habits ought to go away. There are two ways to do this that the Assembly should consider.

The first would be to encourage and assist citizens in withholding a portion of their tax obligation roughly equal to their share of the cost of the war and spy budgets. The Assembly should have persuaded The National War Tax Resistance Coordinating Committee to join the network of NGOs. This particular NGO is a coalition of local, regional, and national groups supportive of war tax resistance. [http://www.nwtrcc.org] There are several legal ways to keep one's taxable income from being siphoned off for war and spy expenses, and the NGO has over 100 counselors to assist tax resistors in the process. Personally, I must admit that I don't have the courage to try it myself.

The second is to end the U.S. Supreme Court's unconstitutional ruling that corporations are persons and thus entitled to all of the rights accorded real persons by the Constitution. Ending corporate personhood would be easier said than done. Nevertheless, the Assembly ought to consider the various approaches that could be taken. They include amending U.S. or State Constitutions (Congress recently went through the charade of proposing a Constitutional amendment that never happened); changing corporations' state charters (they could also be changed to prohibit war and spy corporations); passing anti-personhood legislation; passing prohibitive local ordinances; taking a test case to the Supreme Court; and petitioning municipal, state, and federal prosecutors as the case applies to prosecute members of the bar and the judiciary whose arguments for corporate personhood result in verdicts favoring corporations. Except for prohibitive local ordinances, which have been passed here and there, pursuing this tactic would be time consuming and probably futile.

5c. Take the Voter Out of Politics

This tactic may seem counterintuitive and the Assembly might reject it, but bear with me for a moment. If and until America collapses one or the other of the party twins will be in the Oval Office and run Congress, and you know what that means, continuous warring and spying.

Politicians and their supporters don't want the wrong kinds of voters at the polls. Consider this candid statement from the late religious right political activist, Paul Weyrich, at a 1980 training session for 15,000 conservative preachers in Dallas (just imagine being cooped up with them): "I don't want everybody to vote. Elections are not won by a majority of the people. They never have been from the beginning of our country. They are not now. As a matter of fact, our leverage in the elections quite candidly goes up as the voting populace goes down." [29]

208

The Constitution's idiotic stipulation of an Electoral College followed ever since by politicos and their compatriots on the U.S. Supreme Court have thrown up one voting hurdle after another to deter and prevent the wrong kind of voters from voting. The robed injustices, for instance, essentially eviscerated in a 2013 ruling the 1965 Voter Rights Act. Then there is a plethora of other devilish hurdles such as voter ID laws, voter eligibility criteria, and plain old skullduggery such as operatives jamming their opponents" phone banks and vote tampering. Such hurdles plus the self-imposed one of voter apathy largely explain why voter turnout is so low even in presidential elections (54.9% in 2012).

But let's not kid ourselves about two more facts of America's history from Day 1 and never stopping. Voting by the electorate may be the hallmark of a true democracy, but America has always been a fake democracy. Proposing a "don't vote" campaign therefore would not be antidemocratic.

What might happen if the campaign was carried out and succeeded in the 2016 presidential election? Suppose the voter turnout was cut in half. The Republicans would undoubtedly benefit but it could be a pyrrhic victory. The no-vote majority would have sent a vote of no confidence and disgust that would surely stun and might even shame the party twins to scale back their enthusiasm for all things military and spy related. What do you think? My present inclination is to sit out the 2016 election with my own personal no-vote campaign.

5d. Try Deliberative Democracy

A model political system known as deliberative democracy appeared in 1980 that calls for selection of a representative sample of the public to deliberate an issue such as warring and spying and then to conduct a poll among themselves to choose a public policy option. [30] The results can be used to inform public officials on the issue and sometimes is a stand-in for a traditional vote on the issue. Political scientist professor and philosopher James Fishkin has written about numerous applications in the U.S. and elsewhere of the deliberative democracy process. [31] The Assembly's political alliance could try to implement the model nationwide. A major shortcoming of this approach, however, is that the outcome of the deliberations is fed to the party twins.

5e. Try Federal Ballot Initiatives

A different variation of deliberative democracy is the idea of "direct decrees" by the people as expressed in federal ballot initiatives. Many states already have ballot initiatives, but an amendment to the U.S. Constitution would be required to implement federal ballots, so this tactic would be a long shot at best.

That ends the tactics in Step 5. Before going on to Step 6, though, let's look at three tactics that should be avoided as part of Step 5; revolution, secession, and physically challenging the war and spy industries.

America's Declaration of Independence allows the "People to alter or to abolish it, and to institute new Government, laying its foundation on such principles and organizing its powers in such form, as to them shall seem most likely to effect their Safety and Happiness." Thomas Jefferson called for periodic revolutions, but I don't think he meant a word of it anymore than did that provision in the Declaration. Jefferson and his fellow framers were far more anti-revolutionary than revolutionary in their views on how to govern the new nation. [32]

I don't recommend even a peaceful revolution like Vaclav Havel's "Velvet" revolution. He called for a peaceful uprising in the former Czechoslovakia, whose citizens were oppressed by a totalitarian Communist regime. Peaceful demonstrations by small groups of students, artists, and scientists were followed by massive demonstrations, a general strike, the major media's decision to join the general strike, and negotiations with the Communist-controlled government that subsequently acceded to a new government led by Mr. Havel." [33] The risk of emulating the Velvet Revolution is that the war and spy gang would turn it into a bloodbath.

I should add here that Leah Bolger, retired U.S. Navy Commander and subsequently heavily involved in the antiwar movement, disagrees with my opposition to "even a peaceful revolution." "Massive protests," she says, "are an important component, but massive acts of civil disobedience would be exponentially more effective. Even small acts of civil disobedience can be very effective." [Personal communication] My view is that civil disobedience is no substitute for carrying out a strategic and comprehensive plan like the one I have proposed. If done well, there would eventually be no more warring and spying.

211

The second tactic is a drastic one, secession from the Union. It actually happened once, you remember, when eleven Southern States seceded in the run up to the Civil War. The US Supreme Court seems ambivalent about whether secession would be constitutionally legal. [34] Nevertheless, the aim of the Assembly should be to end the Union's warring and spying without ending the Union.

The third tactic involves engaging in physical protests against the war and spy industries. The protests are futile. The industries will continue doing their business as usual as long as they have Uncle Sam as an insatiable shopper. And protests can be dangerous. Vietnam veteran Brian Willson knows from first-hand experience. [35] He stepped onto the railroad tracks at Concord Naval Weapons Station in Northern California determined to stop trains carrying arms bound for U.S. wars in Central America. Along came a U.S. Navy train at three times the railroad speed limit and hit Mr. Wilson, cracking his skull, sheering off a leg and leaving the other dangling.

Mr. Wilson miraculously survived. He is a hero of mine. Besides being a brave peace activist who continues his activism, he is a lawyer and writer.

Step 6. Converting the War and Spy Industries

As Ellen Hodgins Brown, lawyer and prolific book and article writer notes, "If we had peace, the war machine would be out of a job." [36] She goes on to tell about how the military and the war industry can be civilianized. She gives as examples turning bases into industrial parks, schools, airports, hospitals, and recreation facilities; and converting factories that churn out war machines into factories producing consumer and capital goods such as machine tools, electric locomotives, farm machinery, oil field equipment, and construction machinery for modernizing infrastructure.

Turning swords into ploughshares is an old idea and one that has worked temporarily in the past. At the end of WWII, for example, a large portion of America's GDP was converted from military to civilian outputs.

It has been shown that a well-designed military conversion program can create more jobs, not less than the military can create. Moreover, the war government actually deprives the civilian economy of civilian jobs. [37] Successful conversion would avoid throwing millions of trained people out of work.

The Assembly should promote a "swords to ploughshares" program and offer to help war and spy contractors to make the conversion, telling them the obvious, that if the government converts to a peacetime budget, corporations in the wartime industries will flounder and fail if they don't convert.

I made this very point in a recent book I wrote on what corporations should do if and when government handouts, including "warfare welfare" were to stop. [38] Corporations and those in the war and spy industries are no exception, are poorly managed and poorly organized. The Assembly needs to tell them about my model corporation that they should adopt either before and definitely as the wartime budget starts shriveling.

Companies like those listed in Appendix C are redeemable. The people in them are redeemable. Who knows how many of them feel morally compromised by their work as did Brandon Troy, who courageously and voluntarily resigned from General Dynamics? [39] But whatever their moral stance may be, they are trained and skilled. Rather than being left to fend for themselves, they need to be given peacetime employment opportunities.

Step 7. Launch Your "We/Me Democracy Power"

I don't mean to be presumptuous, impertinent, or preachy, but this last step is for you. But it is also for me and everyone   else   who   reads   this   book.

If you agree that America's warring and spying habits are real and dangerous, what can you do about it? I suggest you launch your "we/me democracy power" by getting yourself involved, if you aren't already, both as an individual (the "me") and as a member of one or more groups(the"we").

You could first share this book with people you know. I'm not suggesting they buy the book. I don't want to make any money off the back of America's misery.

You could review the first six steps and see what you could do to get involved in one or more of them. For example, you could sign every antiwar petition that comes your way. If you know any influential people encourage them to help create the Citizens' Assembly for Peace If you belong to an antiwar NGO encourage it to do the same. You could try to drum up support for the Peace Coalition. And you could use your ingenuity to think of other ways to launch your "we/me democracy power." After all is said and done, the first six steps can't happen if people like you don't get involved. That is why I wrote thisbook.

Endnotes

1. Bumback, GB. The Devil's Marriage: Breaking Up the Corpocracy or Leave Democracy in the Lurch. Author House,2011,185-192.

2. Eisler, R. The Real Wealth of Nations: Creating a Caring Economics. San Francisco: Berrett-Koehler, 2007, 96.

3. Maslow, A. Motivation and Personality. Harper, 1954.

4. Brumback, GB. The Corpocracy and Megaliio's Turn Up Strategy. Democracy Power Press (Kindle Edition), 2012.

5. Wittner, LS. (Edited by John Feffer). How the Peace Movement Can Win. Foreign Policy in Focus Online, April24,2007.

6. Corseri, G. Resurrecting the Anti-war Movement Interview with Gareth Porter by Gary Corseri. Dissident Voice, October 29, 2012.

7. DoD, Defense Contract Dollars by Congressional Districts (109th Congress), USA, 2006, http://geocommons.com/overlays/137.

8. Nader, R. Enlist the Enlightened Super-Rich! HuffPostPolitics, March, 29, 2013.

9. Agencies. Netanyahu Urged y Retired Security Staff to Make Peace. Daily Sabah, November 4, 2014.

10. Zinn, H. A People's History of the United States. Harper Perennial, 2005 (first published in 1980), Chapter 23,632-641.

11. Herman, C. Court Decision: U.S. "Government Agencies" Found Guilty in Martin Luther King's Assassination. Global Research, June 10, 2014.

12. Nader, R. Op. Cit. See also, Nader, R. The Seventeen Solutions: Bold Ideas for Our American Future. New York: Harper Paperback, 2012; and Nader, R. Damaging

Our Country from Wars of Choice. Dissident Voice, September18,2014.

13. Drone Strikes Widely Opposed: Global Opinion of Obama Slips, International Policies Faulted. Pew Global Research Center, June 13, 2012; and Newman, P. Americans are Down on America. Yahoo Finance, July 8, 2014.

14. Zeese, K. & Flowers, M. Crowdsourcing Our Way Out Of the Crisis of Democracy. Popular Resistance, July 13, 2014.

15. Danaher, K, 10 Reasons to Abolish the IMF and World Bank. New York: Seven Stories Press, 1999, 20.

16. Anna, C. Tiny Pacific Nation Sues 9 Nuclear-Armed Powers. Associated Press, April 24, 2014.

17. Sirota, D. What Happened to the Anti-War Movement? Nation of Change, September 6, 2013.

18. Amster, R. The Streets Are Alive With The Sound Of Movement. PopularResistance.Org Daily Digest, December8,2014.

19. E-mail, January 3, 2013, from Debra Sweet, subject: "The World Can't Wait. Stop the crimes of your government.www.worldcantwait.net

20. Ferrechio, S. Pelosi: Bush Impeachment `Off the Table.' The New York Times, November 8, 2006.

21. Sullivan, A. Vermont Towns Vote to Arrest Bush and Cheney. Reuters, March 5, 2008.

22. Levine, S. Republican Voters Want To Impeach The President. Good Luck With That. The Huffington Post, July26,2014.

23. The National Impeachment Resource Center is under the auspices of the blogsite, War Is A Crime.org.

24.RussellTribunal.Wikipedia.

25. Ridley, Y. Bush Convicted of War Crimes in Absentia. Foreign Policy Journal, January 15, 2013.

26. Ross, S. Recommendations From Bush War Crimes Prosecution Conference. WarIsACrime.org.

27. Amato, T. Grand Illusion: The Myth of Voter Choice in a Two Party Tyranny. NY: The New Press, 2009.

28.National War Tax Resistance Coordinating Committee.http://www.nwtrcc.org

29. Neas, RG. The New Face of Jim Crow: Voter Suppression in America. A Special Report. People for the American Way Foundation, August, 2006. www.pfaw.org.

30. Bessette, J. "Deliberative Democracy: The Majority Principle in Republican Government," in Goldwin, RA & Schambra, WA. How Democratic is the Constitution? Washington, D.C., AEI Press, 1980, 102–116.

31. Fishkin, JS. When the People Speak: Deliberative Democracy and Public Consultation. NY: Oxford University Press, 2009.

32. See, e.g., Hermann, B. Eight Counter-revolutionary Founders. Dissident Voice, December 4, 2014; also, Horne, G. The Counter-Revolution of 1776: Slave Resistance and the Origins of the United States of America. New York University Press, 2014.

33. Havel, V. et al. The Power of the Powerless: Citizens Against the State in Central-Eastern Europe. NY: M.E. Sharpe,1985.

34. McClanahan, B. Withdrawal from the Union may be Overkill, but America is Not "One Nation, Indivisible." The American Conservative, December 7, 2012.

35. Butigan, K. Arms Shipment Protest, 25 Years Later. Dissident Voice, September 6, 2012.

36. Brown, EH. The Military as a Jobs Program: There are More Efficient Ways to Stimulate an Economy. Dissident Voice, June 23, 2011.

37. Dumas, LJ.. Finding the Future: The Role of Economic Conversion in Shaping the Twenty-first Century, in Dumas, LJ (Ed). The Socio-Economics of Conversion from War to Peace., M.E. Sharpe, 1995, 3-21.

38. Brumback, GB. Op. Cit.,2012.

39. Cowen, M. Rochester Hills War Veteran Who Quit Defense Contractor Job Now Working on Documentary. The Oakland Press, September 18, 2013.

CHAPTER 8
AMERICA'S FUTURE
BLEAKER OR BRIGHTER?

America's "Sadtistics" Today

Corporate America dictates to government
America

Endless wars and other military
interventions

Excessive deterioration of public
infrastructures

Expelled from the U.N. Human Rights
Commission

Frequent domestic gun violence and
fatalities

Government's disregard for international
accords/treaties

Government's failure to promote the
common welfare

Government's inhibition of dissent

Government lawlessness and
unaccountability

Government's surveillance of all citizens

Government's use of torture

Half of public school students live in
poverty

Huge income inequality

High unemployment rate

High rate of overall poverty

Large population of homeless

Large prison population

Lost domestic opportunities from a
$1trillion national security budget

Low life expectancy

Militarized and homicidal police

Millions of financial hardships from
medical bills
Millions of foreclosed homes
Millions of American livelihoods
dependent on warring and spying
Privatization of public services
Racial hatred and violence
Six deaths a day from lack of health
insurance
Surprising but not unexpected blowbacks

Could she get any bleaker? Absolutely, if she doesn't mend her ways and stop her warring and spying that drain her resources, not to mention lives and privacy.

As she sows, so she shall reap. America could sometime in the future reap one or more of at least five fates: a failed state and beyond; armed revolution; escalating blowbacks; Armageddon; and other global calamities. They are not necessarily mutually exclusive or sequential.

Scenario One: A Failed State and Beyond

The non-governmental organization, Fund for Peace (FFP), regularly ranks the nations of the world on its "failed state index." [1] Over 100 nations are put into the "alert" and "warning" categories. The U.S. is not one of them. One reason is that the FFP is politicized. Its biggest funders are the federal government, corporations, and foundations. I suspect another reason is that the government uses FFP to corroborate the picking of nations ripe for "democratization," read that to mean imperialistic subjugation.

Putting the FFP's list aside, there is ample evidence from the list of "sadtistics" that America already is a failed state or close to becoming one. Once an economic superpower, America is on the way to economic ruin according to Dr. Paul Craig Roberts, Assistant Secretary of the US Treasury for Economic Policy in the Reagan Administration. [2]

Scenario Two: Armed Revolution

All of the conditions listed exist today. They are not conjectures about what might happen in the future. What might happen is the very real possibility that if her course is not reversed America may later this century experience widespread public unrest and violence that precipitates an armed revolution (just think of the number of gun carrying citizensinAmerica).

I imagine the Pentagon has a contingency plan to combat armed revolution and is already training for the possibility of it happening. That may be why swarms of Black Hawk helicopters were flying over Minneapolis the summer of 2014.[3]

If an armed revolution were to occur, it would turn into a bloodbath with thousands of the regime's tanks in the streets, Black Hawks and drones overhead and not on training missions, storm troopers, and thuggish, militarized police. The few protestors' deaths during the Vietnam War would be multiplied by the millions. The revolution would probably be followed by a dictatorship, which in turn would eventually deteriorate into a state of dystopia and ultimate collapse. That has happened to a few nation states in the history of civilization and there is no guarantee it won't happen to America.

Scenario Three: Escalating Blowbacks

America was born in the womb of war
Will she die in its arms?
---The author

As I have said, blowback is an exercise in retributive justice, an eye for an eye. There are two sources of blowbacks, or retaliatory actions, one internal involving citizens against their own government, the other external involving actions against a nation by sources outside of it. Both sources produce blowbacks varying in size, intensity, and harm done. By "escalating blowbacks" I mean repeated retaliations against the same target(s) that increase in size, intensity, and harm done. Escalating blowbacks lead to a "mass of bodies for a mass of bodies."

Internal Blowbacks

Internal blowbacks happen probably daily in America. Most are very small scale, as when, for instance, one or a few citizens protest some government action or inaction. A few blowbacks have been of a much larger scale; viz. the Vietnam War protests and the riots following the assassination of the Reverend Dr. Martin Luther King, Jr. Then there was the really monumental blowback with a slight twist, the Civil War.

There has yet to be a military coup against the politicians because the military/intelligence agencies get whatever they want from them. There has yet to be an armed

222

revolution by the masses since the Civil War, and I hope there never will be one.

External Blowbacks

If you agree with the view that the U.S. provoked Japan into bombing Pearl Harbor (see Appendix A) then that "day in infamy" as FDR famously and perhaps deceptively put it, was the most monumental blowback on America ever carried out by another nation---so far. More deadly external blowbacks were to follow years later, some on American soil, some on Americans in foreign countries: the Beirut barracks bombings in 1983, the 1988 bombing of PAA Flight 103 over Lockerbie; the 1993 bombing of the World Trade Center; the downing of TWA Flight 800 in 1996; the 1998 bombings of U.S. embassies in Kenya and Tanzania; the "9/11" attack; the Baltimore marathon bombing in 2013; the beheadings by the ISIS in 2014.

Unless and until America's two habits are kicked more blowbacks are inevitable. But don't take it from me. Take it from some very authoritative people like the following. Note particularly the Rumsfeld report in 2004, which apparently the former Secretary of Defense shelved.

Four-star Marine General James Cartwright, a confidante of President Obama for years warned that U.S. drone strikes "are begging for retaliation." [4]

Richard Falk, UN special rapporteur on human rights in the Palestinian territories, stated after the Boston attack: "The American global domination project is bound to generate all kinds of resistance in the post-colonial world. In some respects, the United States has been fortunate not to experience worse blowbacks. ... We should be asking ourselves at this moment, 'How many canaries will have to die before we awaken from our geopolitical fantasy of global domination?'" [5]

David Kilcullen, former senior advisor to General David Petraeus: the "blowback and the aspect of political destabilization – those things ultimately do make us less safe." [6]

Marisa L. Porges, former counterterrorism adviser in the Departments of Defense and Treasury: "Those who naïvely believed that Osama bin Laden's death and America's forthcoming departure from Afghanistan would usher in a new era free of threats from Al Qaeda have been proved wrong. America's heavy reliance on drones ---may radicalize more people and encourage them to join forces with terrorists — creating more enemies for America, not fewer." [7]

Donald Rumsfeld, when he was Secretary of Defense commissioned in 20044 a study of the causes of terrorism against America. The conclusion: "American direct intervention in the Muslim World has paradoxically elevated the stature of and support for radical Islamists, while diminishing support to single digits in some Arab societies. Muslims do not hate our freedom, but rather they hate our policies." [8]

Pierre Sprey, a former Pentagon official and fighter aircraft designer: "---what happens on the ground is for every one of those impacts [drone strikes] you get five or ten times as many recruits for the Taliban as you've eliminated. [9]

Lawrence Wilkerson, former chief of staff to Secretary of State Colin Powell: "Tell me how we are winning if every time we kill one [by drone strikes], we create 10?" [10]

I believe Mr. Wilkerson's question was rhetorical. I think he knows we are not winning the battle to reduce the probability of blowback. America has created so many enemies. In Pakistan, a country frequently struck by drones, 74% of its populace polled calls America an enemy. [11] Another poll showed widespread disapproval throughout the world of U.S. drones strikes, with only the U.S. and two other countries (Israel and Kenya) showing slim majorities of approval. [12] Finally, recall the poll cited in the second chapter that most of the world considers America to be the greatest threat to the world. America has deservedly become a pariah among nations.

Recall in Chapter 1 my mentioning that America's regimes have carried out over time covert military actions in 134 countries and currently have authorized torture chambers in 54 countries. Every one of those countries is a potential source of external blowback no matter how long ago they suffered at the hands of America. Memories and legends of carnage and suffering rarely fade. Some of those country's despotic regimes, usually put in place as puppet regimes with the help of America's regime have likely allowed U.S. drone strikes as a means to thwart internal rebellion as much if not more so than to thwart external terrorism directed toward the U.S. In Yemen, however, a country with many drone strike casualties, the parliament passed a non-binding resolution to ban the strikes. [13]

The likelihood of external terrorist attacks not only increases with the continued military presence and action of the U.S, but also with advances in technology and ingenuity in its use. The "underwear bomber" on an international flight in 2009 to Detroit showed a bit of clumsy ingenuity that fortunately failed. [14] Can you just imagine a bunch of terrorists brainstorming new techniques and uses? What might they be? I don't even want to think about it, but the regime's brain center (wherever that is) better think about it unless it wants to declare peace to the world. Meanwhile, terrorists can and do retaliate with a simple technique perhaps as old as historyitself,beheading.

America's top military general Martin Dempsey, according to his spokesman, Colonel Ed Thomas, "believes that ISIS is a regional threat that will soon become a threat to the United States and Europe." Thomas then added, "He (Dempsey) believes that ISIS must be pressured both in Iraq and in Syria." [15] As Thomas was speaking the U.S. was raining bombs on Iraq to counteract the ISIS and who knows what was being done to Syria. Not too many weeks later President Obama accelerated his drone attacks and other military operations to "degrade and destroy the ISIS." [16]

General Dempsey's premonitions may be borne out sooner than later. According to a U.S. counter-terror official, the FBI on November 30, 2014 warned the U.S. military that "ISIS members are "spotting and assessing" individuals in the U.S. who they believe may be interested in carrying out attacks on U.S. soil against members of the U.S. military."[17]

ISIS is a good example of blowback in retaliation for U.S. military interventions in the Greater Middle East. An expert on that region, Graham Fuller, a former CIA analyst for 30 years, believes that "---the United States is one of the key creators of this organization. The United States did not plan the formation of ISIS, but its destructive interventions in the Middle East and the war in Iraq were the basic causes of the birth of ISIS." [18]

My belief on this matter is that the origin, growth and increasing threat of ISIS could very well be a harbinger of a very different and final D-Day, dooms-day, which leads us in a moment to the fourth scenario. What is so worrisome because it is so very possible if not probable is that other countries and terrorist groups will start using their own or hijacked drones to obliterate their enemies, and America could someday be at the top of their hit list. Drone authority and peace activist Medea Benjamin expressed that very worry in her book on drones and drone warfare that I cited in the Preface. [19]

Scenario Four: Armageddon

Armageddon may someday be a reality, not just a scriptural prophecy. Humanity has had the capacity for total self-destruction ever since America introduced nuclear bombs to the world. Armageddon could happen by accident rather than by intent, and there have indeed been several "near misses."

In his book, Command and Control, Eric Schlosser studied nuclear accidents on American soil. He found that the U.S. government lied about, covered up, and underreported these accidents. He thinks it is inevitable that there will be more nuclear accidents within our own borders. [20] I think the probability is even higher that America's nuclear warheads will explode well beyond her borders since the U.S. and Israel reportedly have contingency plans for a nuclear attack on Iran. [21]

Armageddon could easily happen if there were escalating blowbacks or confrontations among one or more warriors-in-chief and one of them had the mentality of the late General Curtis Lemay, who seriously proposed dropping "the entire stockpile of atomic bombs in a single massive attack" on the Soviet Union during the cold war. [22] Then there was the former Secretary of State Henry Kissinger who called a high-level nuclear alert in 1973 to "warn the Russians not to interfere in the ongoing Israel-Arab war and, in particular, not to interfere after he had informed the Israelis that they could violate a ceasefire the U.S. and Russia had just agreed upon." [23]

Nine countries thereabout currently possess nuclear weapons. [24] Not all of them have signed a treaty agreeing to discontinue expanding their nuclear weapon capability. The U.S. has the most adversarial relations with three of those nations, China, North Korean, and Russia. Sometimes the disputes become overheated and high-level warnings by one or both parties are issued. Whether these verbal exchanges would ever culminate in an exchange of nuclear bombs hurling back and forth remains to be seen. Some pundits argue that U.S. militarism is heading it toward WWIII. [25]

Scenario Five:
Ecocide, Genocide and Manufactured Plague

Three other potential calamities for the human race that also, like hurling ballistic war heads, transcend nation state borders are ecocide, genocide and manufactured plague.

Mother Nature may have the last laugh, or blowback, if we don't start placating her instead of plucking her. The planet, offering finite, not infinite resources for human use and having exceeded its carrying capacity for nearly seven billion humans and counting almost exponentially, could very well become unlivable eventually with air that is unbreathable, with soaring temperatures that are unbearable, with water that is undrinkable, with food that is toxic, and with no oil to lubricate and combust. Before those extreme conditions there very likely would be an outbreak of "resource wars." [26] And we can "depend" on our military being in the thick of it.

Genetic engineering, the military discovered, could make its arsenal of biological weapons more effective by genetically altering them. [27] Since there are very few natural pathogens that lend themselves to biological warfare, the genetic engineering of unnatural pathogens is where the military is apparently staking its future in remaining a superpower and threat to uncooperative nations. The military's secretive research arm, DARPA (Defense Advanced Research Project Agency), has launched an expensive program called "Living Foundaries," a misleadingly innocent name if there ever was one. "Think of it," says journalist and editor Katie Drummond, "like an assembly line, but one that would churn out modified biological matter — man-made organisms — instead of cars or computer parts." [28] Just think, too, of what might happen if a psychopathic warrior-in-chief, unrestrained military and political advisors, and mad scientists all came together to plot and unleash an explosion of unnatural pathogens on their adversaries. Can't you just picture it next century; our one-eyed, two-headed, three-legged species walking down the street, if any streets are left?

The recent scare of a spreading Ebola epidemic has heightened concerns about biological warfare and Ebola terrorism in particular. A journalist writing in Scientific American reports that "National security and infectious disease experts agree the obstacles to a large-scale assault with Ebola are formidable." She concludes that "---the possibility of rogue organizations sowing this terror on a similar scale seems largely out of reach." [29] But the journalist and the experts may be too sanguine. Several readers using their imagination in commenting on the article described some very plausible and easy ways for suicide carriers of Ebola to "carry" it to populated areas.

That journalist, moreover, apparently was not referring to any "rogue organizations" in America deliberately manufacturing a plague in various parts of the world. If the following news item is authentic there should never be any doubt about how fiendish an American regime can be. Dr. Cyril Broderick, a Liberian scientist and a former professor of Plant Pathology at the University of Liberia's College of Agriculture and Forestry, claims that the US Department of Defense had been funding Ebola trials on humans in Guinea and Sierra Leone just weeks before the Ebola outbreaks there. [30] This claim obviously warrants follow up as the situation develops.

There you have it, five bleaker than bleak scenarios for America's future. One or more of them is bound to happen if America does not mend her ways. And that is not likely to happen in the foreseeable future. According to investigative journalist Glenn Greenwald, "key Democrats, led by Hillary Clinton, leave no doubt that endless war is official U.S. doctrine." [31]

Well, I have no doubt that America's endless wars are her birthmark. She was born in the womb of war; will she die in her arms? Or will she become an "Alter America?" The answer depends on whether millions of Americans can be united and organized to end America's "oldest professions." I see no hope for America's future if the actions proposed in the previous chapter or ones like them arenottaken.

In his book, Dirty Wars, Jeremy Scahill, tells his readers that the stories in his book "reveal a haunting vision of what our future holds for us in a world gripped by ever-expanding dirty wars." [32] Mr. Scahill, my having grandchildren makes me super sensitive to that vision.

The Doomsday Clock

The Bulletin of Atomic Scientists is an international group of world renowned scientists who have been publishing the "Doomsday Clock" since 1947 to symbolize the perils posed by nuclear weapons and climate change." [33] "Midnight" represents the time when doomsday begins. In 2007 the clock was moved from 7 to 5 minutes to midnight because of the potential catastrophe from 27,000 nuclear weapons in the world, with 2,000 of them ready to launch, and the destruction of human habitats from climate change. Doomsday has now ticked closer with the clock having been set at 3 minutes to midnight in January 2015.

Endnotes

1. Fund for Peace. The Failed State Index. http://www.ffp.statesindex.org/rankings-2013-sortable.
2. Roberts, P.C. Ruin Is Our Future. OpEdNews, January 16, 2015.
3. Rupar, A. Downtown Minneapolis Invaded by Black Hawk Helicopters. [Tue.]Minneapolis City Pages, August 28,2012.
4. Dreyfuss, B. General Cartwright Warns of Drone 'Blowback' The Nation, March 22, 2013.
5. Falk, R. A Commentary on the Marathon Murders. Foreign Policy Journal, April 21, 2013
6. Huffington, A. 'Signature Strikes' and the President's Empty Rhetoric on Drones. Huffington Post, July 10, 2013.

7. Porges, ML. Dead Men Share No Secrets. The New York Times, September 24, 2012.

8. Greenwald, G. A Rumsfeld-Era Reminder about What Causes Terrorism. Salon, October 20, 2009.

9. See Bill Moyers Journal . Pierre Sprey and Marilyn Young. PBS, June 30, 2009.

10. Huffington, Op Cit.

11. Pew Research Global Attitudes Project. Pakistani Public Opinion Ever More Critical of U.S.: 74% Call America an Enemy. Pew Research Center, June 27, 2012.

12. Drake, B. Report Questions Drone Use, Widely Unpopular Globally, But Not In the U.S. Pew Research Center, October 23, 2013.

13. Almasmari, H. Drone Strikes Must End, Yemen's Parliament Says. CNN World, December 15, 2013.

14. Bunkley, N. Would-Be Plane Bomber Is Sentenced to Life in Prison. The New York Times, February 17, 2012.

15. IS Will 'Soon' Pose Threat to US: Top General. Yahoo News, August 25, 2014.

16. Cohn, M. Obama Declares Another Illegal War. www.truthout.org. September 19, 2014.

17. Brown, P. & Sciutto, J. FBI Warns Military of ISIS Threat. CNN Politics, December 1, 2014.

18. Basaran, E. Former CIA Officer Says US Policies Helped Create IS. Almonitor, September 2, 2014. See also, Hedges, C. ISIS—the New Israel. Truthdig, December 12, 2014.

19. Benjamin, M. Drone Warfare: Killing by Remote Control. Verso, 2013.

20. Schlosser, E. Command and Control. Penguin Press, 2013.

21. Ross, S. Toward a World War III Scenario: America's "Contingency Plan" to Attack Iran with Nuclear Weapons. Global Research E-Newletter, November 19, 2014.

22. Lashmar, P. Stranger than "Strangelove:" A General's Forays into the Nuclear Zone. Washington Post, July 3, 1994.

23. Noble, S. Anarchy and Near Term Extinction. Dissident Voice, June 18, 2014.

24. Kimball, D. Nuclear Weapons: Who Has What at a Glance. Arms Control Association, June 23, 2014.

25. Boyle, FA. American Militarism Threatening To Set Off World War III. OpEdNews, December, 12, 2012. See also: "Chossudovsky, M. Towards a World War III Scenario: The Dangers of Nuclear War. E-Book Series No. 1.0, Global Research Publishers, 2011; and Roberts, PC. Pushing Toward the Final War. OpEdNews, March 28, 2014.

26. Klare, M. Resource Wars: The New Landscape of Global Conflict. Holt Paperbacks, 2002.

27. Emerging Technologies: Genetic Engineering and Biological Weapons: A Report by the Sunshine Project and Third World Network, 2004.

28. Drummond, K. DARPA, Venter Launch Assembly Line for Genetic Engineering. May 22, 2012, WIRED.

29. Maron, DF. Weaponized Ebola: Is It Really a Bioterror Threat? Scientific American, September 25, 2014.

30. Guzman, TA. U.S. is Responsible for the Ebola Outbreak in West Africa: Liberian Scientist
Global Research, October 17, 2014. See also, Roberts, PC. The Entry of Ebola into the US Has Hallmarks of a Planned Happening. OpEdNews, October 21, 2014.

31. Greenwald, G. Key Democrats, Led by Hillary Clinton, Leave No Doubt that Endless War is Official U.S. Doctrine. The Intercept, October 7, 2014.

32. Scahill, J. Dirty Wars: The World is a Battlefield. Nation Books, 2013. Xxiv.

33. Bulletin of Atomic Scientists. Timeline: It is 3 Minutes to Midnight. January 25, 2015. thebulletin.org/timeline

AFTERWORD

An Afterword is a good place for authors to put down their thoughts that either came after the book's main text is essentially sealed or that do not fit in it very well.

Brainstorming Chapter 7

The seven-step program proposed in Chapter 7 does not specify in detail exactly how each step is to be accomplished and who will be getting it accomplished. Also not included is any timeline with immediate and intermediate objectives and ways to know when those objectives have been met. My own immediate objective, to get this book published, precedes the first step.

Recall that David Swanson wrote in the book's forward that this first step, establishing a Citizens' Assembly for Peace, "is the way to go." I value his opinion because of his credentials and experiences in peace activism. This step and the third one of starting a Peace Coalition are probably the most critical and difficult ones and should thus be given the highest priority. If they cannot be started or if they fail the whole program will fail, and failure does not portend well at all for America's viable future.

More detailed planning obviously needs to be done to spell out how those two steps are to get done and by whom. The planning would definitely benefit from some preliminary brainstorming by people who are prominent peace activists. Toward that end I hope to be able to do some brainstorming with them through e-mails and teleconferences guided by a series of questions.

Here are some illustrative questions that need answered in planning the details for the first step. Are there any peace and antiwar organizations or other potentially relevant and even unrealistic but not impossible organizations (such as, e.g., that 8 million member religious organization I mentioned in Chapter 6) missing from the list in Chapter 7? What about David Swanson's recommendation made in the Forward about expanding a nationwide Citizens' Assembly for Peace into an assembly of citizens of the world? Would that not be a real possibility, given Medea Benjamin has written about the "opposition to drones going global," in her marvelous, very moving and must read book on drone warfare? [1] Who are some nationally prominent individuals who might be coaxed into championing the idea of a Citizen's Assembly for Peace? Should all of the organizations be approached at roughly the same time or should a few of the more affluent ones be approached first and asked to take the lead in recruiting the other organizations (e.g., I believe the American Friends Service Committee has an annual revenue of about $3 million). Should some level of public support for the Assembly be sought first, and, if so, how, (e.g., by an Internet petition drive to collect thousands of supportive signatures to be delivered to the organizations) before contacting the organizations? Are there any wealthy foundations that ought to be contacted about helping to fund the start-up and operation of the Assembly? Should the Assembly have a permanent staff? What should be its qualification requirements? From where will the staff be recruited? And so on.

Those are some questions that come to mind just for the first step. Staring at and thinking about them alone makes the goal of ending America's warring and spying seem unreachable. Maybe it is. But fatalism, or doing nothing, could be fatal in the long run.

Second Thoughts

On Renaming the Citizens' Assembly

"The beginning of wisdom," Confucius said, is to call things by their proper names." I was not very wise in Chapter 7 when I didn't change the name of the "Citizens Assembly for Peace" to the "Citizens' Assembly for Alter America." I am doing so now. The new name helps "connect the dots" of the many single-issue movements in America. The adjective, "alter" also connotes two separate but related ideas, another, different America and the altering or reforming of America that will be required.

On Democracy and the American Revolution

Chapter 2 of my book, The Devil's Marriage, is titled Earlier Corpocracies: A Review [2]. It opens with this "scorecard:"

Scoreboard is Stuck: Corpocracy 5, Democracy 3

> The Crown's Corpocracy (Until 1776)
> Democracy
> The Robber Baron's Corpocracy (1865-1901)
> Democracy
> The Flapper Era Corpocracy (1921-1933)
> Democracy
> The Cold War Era Corpocracy (1950-1970s)
> The Current Corpocracy (1970s-Continuing)

After reading very recently Arthur Robbins compelling book about "democracy denied" I realized that my scorecard was totally wrong. It should read Corpocracy 238 years, Democracy 0 years. [3] I already knew that the Greek origin of the word, "democracy" combines two

Greek words standing for people and power. What I had failed to realize until reading Dr. Robbins book is that not only has there never been a democracy in the entire history of America there has never been a democracy in the history of the entire world. The closest brush people in new America had with democracy were people living in the Common Wealth of Pennsylvania with its own Constitution of 1776 that preceded the defeat of any true form of democracy by the aristocrats who wrote the new nation's Constitution.

Just think of that. When I was young I was taught that ancient Greece was the crucible of America's democracy. That is sheer hokum fed to us by America's power elite, our government, our educators, and by about everybody else who might be considered opinion makers or propagandists or outright liars. It is all hokum on a massive scale, the likes of which have probably never happened elsewhere in the world.

Not even during the so-called halcyon era of democracy when Pericles ruled Greece did she have a democracy. Only about one-tenth of Athens' populace was officially designated citizens. Slaves, women, and men who had not served in the military were all non-citizens. Military service was an absolute necessity since Pericles presided over the remaining years of the war with Persia and the first few years of the 30 year war between Athens and Sparta.

Another very recent eye-opener for me on the true origins of America was learning about history professor Gerald Horne and his book on how the American Revolution was precipitated in no small measure by the colonists' fear, especially that of the wealthy and privileged ones, of their slaves, emboldened by the prospect of slavery being abolished in Britain, would revolt and be joined by an influx of slaves who had been revolting in Jamaica and Antigua. [4]

What are we to make of the foregoing accounts of the myth of democracy and the origin of the American Revolution coupled with what I have already written about America's beginning and her conduct ever since? Do they all add up to an inglorious ending of America some day? They will I predict unless a majority of Americans can be persuaded to insist on rebuilding America along the lines of the model of Alter Model, starting with the abolition of America's warring and spying.

On America's Split Personality and Its Implications

I learned recently what really shouldn't have surprised me, namely, that 51% of Americans approve of the CIA's torture program. [5] Can we count them as the half of America's personality that is sociopathic? Maybe yes, maybe not. I'm not a "cultural psychiatrist." What I think can be said accurately is that our government scared the wits out of those witless people and that they, along with the majority of Americans who approve of President Obama's drone hit lists (probably the same people) are a lost cause in so far as persuading them to believe this book and embrace and act upon the proposals in Chapter 7.

I also learned even more recently that of the 1000 Americans responding to a Gallop poll taken in 2014 only twenty-one percent said they were dissatisfied with their "freedom to choose what to do with your life." [6] This finding suggests that the majority of Americans' personalities can be characterized charitably as "close minded."

On Secession

I am having second thoughts about secession. While I rejected this tactic in Chapter 7 I am now warming to the idea of it even though it may never come to pass. Big government is exactly what the aristocratic founders of our nation wanted and for the same reasons that prevail today, to grow the empire. From now on I am going to advocate dissolving central, nationalized government and replacing it with separate and independent regionalized governments.

On the Two Major Roadblocks to World Peace

Arguably the two most roguish nations on our planet, the U.S. and Israel, are the two major roadblocks to world peace. [7] I have dealt with the first extensively in this book already. Now I return briefly to the controversial relationship between these two nations.

There are opposite explanations for the controversy. One says Israel has the upper hand through its powerful lobbying group in America, the American Israel Public Affairs Committee, or AIPAC. [8] The other says essentially that the U.S. corpocracy since Israel's statehood, has exploited it as a proxy excuse to keep control of the resource rich Greater Middle East. [9]

I favor the second explanation simply for two reasons. One, I think it is preposterous to think that the world's superpower would be any tiny nation's lap dog, the U.S. neocon's bias toward Israel at all costs notwithstanding. Israel is tiny but it is strategically important to the U.S. corpocracy, a dependency not wasted on the neocons. Israel's strategic importance to the U.S., for instance, is why our government funnels more of our money to the

Israel military budget than Israeli citizens spend on it themselves. [10] Two, there never was any great affection to say the least between America's politicians and the general public and Israel before her statehood and the relationship between the two nations' regimes since has been episodic and mutually exploitative.

I will give you several pieces of supportive, absolutely shameful and unforgivable evidence that both the Roosevelt administration along with the British government passed up several opportunities first to allow Hitler to deport all Jews before starting the Holocaust and then to intervene once it was started. Preventing or stopping the Holocaust was simply not a U.S or U.K priority.

Professor Alexander J. Groth, for example, himself a Holocaust survivor, wrote a meticulously researched book with the conclusion that Churchill and Roosevelt were "accomplices" in the Holocaust. Groth says that the two leaders: "refused to protest publically the Holocaust; refused to "commit even one soldier, one plane or one warship to any forcible opposition to the Nazi extermination of the Jews; and they obstructed Jewish escape from Hitler's Europe." [11]

Then there is Nobel Peace Laureate and Holocaust survivor Eli Weise. He contends that: "The greatest tragedy in history could have been prevented had the civilized world spoken up, taken measures in 1939, '40, '41, '42. Each time, in Berlin, Geobbels and the others always wanted to see what would be the reaction in Washington and London and Rome, and there was no reaction so they felt they could continue." [12]

240

Now let's consider "The Riegner Telegram." Gerhardt Riegner was Secretary of the World Jewish Congress in Geneva. Reigner had learned from an authoritative source that Hitler was going to have every Jew in Europe exterminated with Prussic acid. [13] Reigner frantically raced to tell the American Vice Consul in Geneva, Switzerland. The message was eventually passed along to the U.S. State Department in August of 1942. What happened next, hem hawing and resistance within the Roosevelt Administration, including its State Department, was predictable. Much of the American public, its opinion leaders, and government officials, including those in the State Department were prejudiced against the Jews. [14]

But it really doesn't matter which explanation or some other alternative is right. The Greater Middle East will continue to be an explosive cauldron and precursor to WWIII unless the U.S. withdraws its overbearing military presence and deadly military operations in that area.

In the Afterword of The Devil's Marriage I wrote that; "The road to peace for America will have to go through the Middle East." [15] An editorial in The New York Times in 2008 raised the question of "where do we go from here" in that region? [16] My answer was published as "an all editors' selection" for being among the "most interesting and thoughtful comments that represent a range of views."

Here was my answer: "The question needs to be broadened and five answers courageously debated. How can the U.S. stop alienating the Middle East and thereby provoking unnecessary threats not only to us but also to that region? This question should constantly be on the table for serious diplomatic discussion. The first answer, persuade Israel through incentives and appeals to

241

international harmony to return the land acquired in the 1967 war. Second, tell the Palestinians we will help them build their new state if they ask us. Three, renounce our dependence on oil and feverishly develop alternative sources of energy. Four, stop subsidizing our defense industry. Five, stop acting aggressively and unilaterally and start acting peacefully, diplomatically, and multilaterally through a strengthened UN and a reoriented and revitalized State Department wholeheartedly supported by the president and Congress. Ever happen? Let's hope so. Future generations blameless for our inactions and bad actions today deserve a world we ought to be rebuilding for their arrival into whatever faith, culture, and nationality they may be born. Peace, Shalom, Salam."

Having now thought through and written this section I think my seven step program should be modified to include as a centerpiece strategy implementation of my proposal published by the New York Times.

On Crime and Punishment

I'm plainly no Dostoevsky but I do know the truism that punishment should fit the crime. I can think of a few instances in my lifetime where the fit was locked tight and final. Hitler, for one, executed himself. Ten of his henchmen were given the death penalty by the judges at the Nuremburg trials and hanged. Mussolini was killed by some fellow Italians and then hung upside down for public viewing.

Those instances represented an eye for an eye so to speak, or retributive justice. But must the "table of penalties" always be level with the "table of crimes? No, not if you subscribe to my human equation and its implications for punishment, and if you are willing to set aside the innocuous biblical entreaties about forgiveness; we must, if we are going to be evenhanded and just, take the criminals' badvantages into account as "mitigating" factors, so to speak.

So where does the above paragraph lead us? It leads me anyway to the unofficial international war criminals Bush and Obama and their chieftains instrumental in all of the deaths overviewed in the first and second chapters. In my seventh chapter I wrote that; "The Assembly's litigation group needs to leave no stone unturned in finding and/or devising ways to proceed to nail the criminals through impeachment and/or prosecution and conviction."

I am tempted now to modify that proposal a bit given that the criminals have so solidly shielded themselves from accountability. That shield will be difficult if not impossible to crack open. As an alternative a highly prominent and ballyhooed citizen's tribunal ought to be created by or independently of the Assembly. The tribunal would review the evidence against the criminals and publicly announce their verdict and sentencing. In determining the sentencing the tribunal would compare the enormity of the crimes committed by the Nazi officials with those committed by the Bush and Obama regimes. The tribunal would take all extenuating circumstances (i.e., the badvantages and insanity if judged to be the case) into consideration in its sentencing decision and would not rule out the possibility of some form of conditional amnesty. The tribunal's findings and decisions would be widely publicized and obviously sent to the criminals with a request that they vacate their offices. The public would be invited to submit endorsements.

Would such a symbolic tactic produce any dramatic effect such as galvanizing the public into further action or shaming the officials into resignation? I don't know, but it needs to be tried.

The less symbolic tactic I mentioned in Chapter 7 of emulating those Vermont town councils that voted Bush and Cheney persona non grata, on second thought here, ought to be given greater priority than I gave it in that chapter.

On Civil Resistance

Since writing Chapter 7 I have been doing some more reading and thinking about how social movements can eventually lead to significant social changes in a society. As a result, I no longer am opposed to lawful civil resistance as a means to achieving social changes.

The dramatic swing over a decade or so that took place in public opinion toward same-sex marriage could not have happened without the accumulative effect of civil resistance on the part of different sectors of the public. [17] Slowly, as public opinion began changing, the pillars of opposition to same sex marriage and LGBT rights in general began crumbling. These were the pillars that had been erected by politicians, the legal community, the military, some religious leaders, the mainstream media, the entertainment industry, and even the corporate sector at large.

My embrace now of lawful civil resistance as a means to "change the minds and hearts" of the American people leads me to deemphasize certain tactics proposed in Chapter 7 such as those described in reforming the political party system and to place a greater priority on

244

tying the tactics of lawful civil resistance to the tactics described in starting the peace coalition.

On Organized Religion as an Ally of Peace

Were it not for its record of either engaging in war, promoting it or acquiescing to it, one would think organized religion would be a natural ally of and prominent activist for peace. There are, to be sure, some exceptions among the various denominations or religious sects (e.g., the Quakers and the Mennonites), and small religious, antiwar groups can be found protesting now and then, here and there. Overall, though, and throughout history organized religion has been an ally of war, not peace. That is why I included it in Chapter 6 as a "habit helper."

At the same time, however, there are coalitions of major organized religions that just may present an opportunity to be an ally of peace and to shape behavior toward being a habit breaker. With that thought in mind I recently wrote the leaders of the National Council of Churches, USA; the World Council of Churches; the National Council of Synagogues, USA; the Rabbis for Human Rights; and the U.S. Council of Muslim Organizations. They provide overall leadership and guidance for member religious organizations whose memberships total over 180 million Americans.

I told them that any serious antiwar effort must be one of escalating confrontation of the leaders of war. Timidity, pleading, compromise or any of the other conciliatory and conventional approaches to ruling regimes will absolutely fail as they always have. Even mice know better than to sit down at the table with cats.

I also told them that the effort must focus first on the war and spy complex in the U.S. There clearly can be no world peace if militarism is not subdued in the nation that is perceived and correctly so by the rest of the world as the greatest threat to world peace.

I then suggested for their prayerful consideration the following outline for a strategy of escalating confrontation:

1. Create an interreligious task force to plan in detail a strategy for peace, oriented first toward the U.S.
2. Establish a steering council, pick leadership, obtain funding and recruit staff.
3. Help unite the dozens of movements protesting all sorts of different injustices. Connect the dots for these people-- no injustice can really end if war doesn't end. Give the coalition an inspirational and galvanizing name.
4. Warn the leaders of the warring and spying complex in America that the grand movement and its leaders are serious in their intent and actions and are not simply posturing.
5. As an interreligious entity morally and publically condemn the current administration, Congress, the war and spy industries, the mass media, and Hollywood.
6. Unleash a torrent of escalating litigation. The first would be a rehearsal in which a prestigious group of Americans conducts a Tribunal Court ending in the informal prosecution and conviction of all US international war criminals. Follow up by compelling the International Criminal Court to prosecute all U.S. international war criminals even though the U.S. regime refuses to join the ICC.
7. Promote and engage in all forms of lawful civil resistance coupled with organized rallies of millions of protesters in the four regions of the US.

8. Monitor progress. If there is little to none, don't despair. Try a Plan B. We must be good and responsible ancestors of future generations. For their sake we must not fail.

What do you think will be their responses?

Tweets for Peace

In just a few years I have posted over 2500 tweets. I have listed below some of them mostly on war and peace and without the 140 character limitation requiring abbreviations and other shortcuts. The tweets have not been organized into subcategories.

People tend to remember and react more to shorter than to longer messages. That's why at the end of each chapter of my Devil's Marriage book I put a list of "memory ticklers and one-liners." [18] It's also why I wrote the humorous book, Party Politics: Don't Get Caught Speechless. [19] And it's why I am listing the tweets here.

While I hope you remember and act on what you read in the rest of the book, I also hope these tweets will be memorable ones that might come in handy in conversations about war and peace.

Some of the Tweets

World Communion Day. What's desperately needed before too late is a worldwide communion of activists demanding peace
Future of America? Ask War Lord and its Bible of Death
Ebola and Warola. See any connection? I do
If only humans were animals They don't massacre their own kind

247

Roadblocks to peace: politicians-military-defense industry-you and I.

Politicians-military-defense industry can't stop warring. They are addicted to it.

Election 2014 didn't matter. Party Twins both are pawns of corporations and the war and spy industries

There's a Veterans FOR Peace Let's unite, act against war and someday be Veterans OF Peace.

Honor vets, dishonor war

The mother of war is war

Bring home the troops permanently and not in caskets

Let's link arms against arms

Arms are for hugging (borrowed from Code Pink)

The corpocracy has the upper hand. Let's unite & give it our back hand

US stop $billions on R&D for exotic weapons against people Start R&D on "weapons" against quakes, canes, tornados, and climate damage

Time to make corpocracy a corpsocracy

RAW=WAR backwards. War's a raw deal for everybody but politicians and those in the war business

Congress in session. An un-American activity?

Pol ecat, Pol itician Get the drift?

Fight for peace alone and lose. Unite and win

Socio pathological war culture: Make war. Glorify war. Memorialize war dead

Obama's secret kill list: Nation's top Mafia boss?

Turn peace, not war into a profit

America won't be endless if its wars are

Schizophrenia: Pro-life and Pro-U.S. Wars in the same brain

US spends more killing foreigners than developing America's youth. Does that make moral/economic sense?

Born in the womb of war. Will America die in her arms?

The poverty of peace. The profligacy of war. The passivity and powerlessness of the people

Peace thru strength? Never. Strength always slams the door shut

Pearl Harbor: A harbor of death that needn't have happened between two imperialistic rivals

America's Valentine to world: We'll keep killing you till you love us

Military/industrial/political trio on autopilot, drone pun intended

Kindness; word seen by the blind, heard by the deaf.

The real lifers, political careerists not in prison but probably should be

Government polices all but itself, corporations, and the war and spy business

America's sadtistics: Depressing and don't lie about state of our union

Blood spilled by U.S. would fill canyons

Warring takes away lives. Spying takes away privacy

Uncle Sam is a chronic Peeping Tom

"Sinonyms:" Spy/Lie/War/Death

Uncle Sam Wants You! (docile and "terrorfied")

Laugh a day keeps how howel movements moving

Banksters, just another name for War Street

War Time=Standard USA Time

Army chaplain on Iraq battlefield: "We bring God to soldiers and them to God"

Warfare welfare: Millions of Americans' livelihoods depend on it; millions of people die from it

Hollywood: reel war and spy

Political/military/industrial/monster a war drunk and running tab on taxpayers' accounts

Mushrooms, like wrongdoing, grow best in the dark. US war monster grows 24/7

Call to all Occupy groups: Unite and Occupy War!

A Final Afterword

The 2014 mid-term elections have come and gone. The Republicans trounced the Democrats. And both Party Twins keep on trouncing America for their own interests. Now we are seeing in early 2015 that America's two habits continue unabated. For instance, at least six people were killed by a U.S. drone in Pakistan before the first week of the New Year was over. [20] The year 2015, writes Charles Pierson, a lawyer and member of the Pittsburgh Anti-Drone Warfare Coalition, "might be even a better year for drones." [21] And Allegra Kirkland, associate managing editor of AlterNet, has some New Year's news for us: "This year, we're on track to spend over $1 trillion on national security,---." [22] On January 20th of this New Year Nick Turse, managing editor of TomDispatch.com and a fellow at the Nation Institute, reported that the U.S. is conducting "a shadow war in 150 countries;" by my count that amounts to the U.S. causing mayhem and death in three fourths of the world's nations. [23] Will it ever end or will it end America? How can we convince the majority of Americans that through their acquiescence, passivity, and paralyzing fear they are inviting a chain of blowbacks to strike America in years to come? Shouldn't America stand for peace, not war?

Endnotes

1. Benjamin, M. Drone Warfare: Killing by Remote Control. Verso, 2013.
2. .Brumback, GB. The Devil's Marriage: Break Up the Corpocracy or Leave Democracy in the Lurch. Author House, 2011, 25-30.
3. Robbins, AD. Democracy Denied: The Untold Story. Acropolis Books, 2014.

4. Horne, G. The Counter-Revolution of 1776: Slave Resistance and the Origins of the United States of America. NYU Press, 2014.

5. Zapata, NH. Study: Over Half of Americans Think CIA Torture Methods Revealed in Senate Report Are Justified. Truthdig, December 18, 2014.

6. Bovard, J. Surrendering Liberty America's Fatal Freedom Apathy. Counterpunch, January 28, 2015.

7. Chomsky, N. The Dangerous Rogue States Operating in the Mideast -- U.S. and Israel.
Alternet, December 4, 2013.

8. See, e.g.,Mearsheimer, J. & Walt, S. The Israel Lobby and U.S. Foreign Policy. Farrar, Straus and Giroux, 2007.

9. See, e.g., Spritzier, J. Power Comes from The American Ruling Class. newdemocracyworld.org, February 23, 2009.

10. Weir, A. US Taxpayers Paid More to Israeli Defense Budget than Israelis. Veteran News Now, September 17, 2012.

11. Groth, AJ. Accomplices: Churchill, Roosevelt and the Holocaust. Peter Lang International Academic Publishers, 2011.

12. Rogin, J. Eli Weise: Why is Assad Still in Powerr? Foreign Policy, April 23, 2012.

13. LeTraunik, E. The Riegner Telegram. The Jewish Magazine, November 2008.

14. Wickipedia. History of Antisemitism in the United States.

15. Brumback, Op. Cit, 188-189.

16. Editorial. Where Do We Go From Here? The New York Times Online, July 7, 2008.

17. See, e.g., Engler, M. & Engler, P. When the Pillars Fall — How Social Movements Can Win More Victories Like Same-Sex Marriage. Waging Non Violence, July 9, 2014.

18. Brumback, GB. OpCit., 2011.

19. Brumback, GB. Party Politics: Don't Get Caught Speechless. Palm Coast, FL: Democracy Power Press (Kindle Edition), 2010.

20. Gosztola, K. In Pakistan, First US Drone Strike of the New Year Kills At Least Six People. The Dissenter, January 5, 2015.

21. Pierson, C. 2014 Was a Good Year For Drones, 2015 Might be Even Better. Counterpunh, January 07, 2015.

22. Kirkland, A. We Are a Chickenhawk Nation, Blindly Worshiping the Military; Wasting Enormous Amounts on Useless Military Hardware. AlterNet, January 9, 2015.

23. Nick Turse, A Shadow War in 150 Countries. Tomgram, January 20, 2015.

APPENDIX A
WARS' LITMUS TESTS

We know why wars happen. And we know that wars throughout history have killed millions upon millions of human beings. We must ask ourselves and we ought to ask our nation's leaders "What on earth could justify such inhumanity to humanity?" If at least one war passes a litmus test for whether it is just or necessary, then the argument that no war can be just or necessary is repudiated. So let's put war, first, some particular wars and then any war, through 13 litmus tests.

1. WWI?

President Woodrow Wilson tried to sell WWI to the American public by calling it "the war to end all wars." His hype didn't work; only 75,000 men volunteered for an Army that needed one million of them. So Wilson was forced to ask Congress to enact conscription to force participation or be imprisoned.

The war was a slaughterhouse. When it was over 10 million men from the U.S. and the other countries involved had died in battle and millions more were disabled; and for what justifiable or necessary cause? There was none. WWI was a result, the late historian Howard Zinn said, of "imperial rivalries, greed for more territory, a lusting for national prestige, the stupidity of revenge, and mediocre leaders [who] had neither the courage nor the will to stop." [1] Let's add another, really big contributing factor; neither the WWI honchos or any other war's big honchos ever have to go into combat.

2. WWII?

While there seems to be unequivocal evidence that the U.S. not only could have avoided entering WWII but was complicit in its happening, we can still ask whether WWII could be considered a just or necessary war. [2] Not according to Zinn, who raised and answered several key questions. Was the U.S. involvement for the rights of nations to independence and self-determination? To save the Jews (recall the Afterword)? Against racism? For democracy? No, not at all according to his review of the evidence; the U.S. involvement in WWII had no such high-minded purposes, and Zinn concluded that "Looking at World War II in perspective, looking at the world it created and the terror that grips our century, should we not bury for all time the idea of just war?" [3]

3. The American Revolution?

America's first war, the American Revolution was fought for the partial right (not everyone was given it) of independence and self-determination. It was a clash between two privileged classes 3,500 miles apart. It did not save the Indians. It led to their decimation and subjugation. It certainly was not against racism. And it certainly was not for a democracy of, for, and by all the people since the "Founding Fathers" were plutocrats and not about to promote the general welfare of everyone living in the new nation. Had the war not been fought British control would have eventually dissipated, just as it eventually lost all of its other colonies, and an America of a less militant nature might have eventually emerged.

4. The Civil War?

The Civil War is the most deadly for Americans of any military interventions launched by a U.S. president. Zinn makes it clear in his writings that President Lincoln provoked the attack on Fort Sumter that launched the Civil War not with the primary purpose of freeing the slaves but to make sure to maintain the ability to expand the nations territory and with it greater markets and resources. Lincoln, in other words, was an early practitioner of imperialism by deadly military means. He was also, I was astonished to learn, a racist if one can take these own remarks of his at face value that he made in a speech he gave in Charleston? "---I am not, nor ever have been, in favor of bringing about in any way the social and political equality of the white and black races---and I as much as any other man am in favor of having the superior position assigned to the white race." [4] Whatever his motives might have been, and whether he spoke with a forked tongue depending on the audience, his decision to start the Civil War was deadly, unnecessary, and morally outrageous. In saying that, I want to make it perfectly clear that I have never in my life been a racist.

If Lincoln had allowed the Confederacy to become a separate nation, slavery would have ended because tenancy was becoming a more practical means of managing agricultural labor, resentment and continued racial discrimination and hatred from forced "emancipation" would have eventually ceased, and there would be two Americas, not one mighty one continuously threatening the world.

5. Self Defense?

Wouldn't a war of self-defense unravel the argument that no war is just or necessary? No, the best defense against modern warfare initiated against the U.S. is prevention through the U.S. having the right kind of foreign policies in place over time. Unfortunately, the administrator of our foreign policy, the Department of State is a subsidiary of the Department of Defense. Our foreign policies are in reality militant military policies.

6. Unavoidable War?

Wouldn't an unavoidable war be just or necessary? No war is unavoidable. A careful reading of the history of U.S. military interventions clearly indicates that all could have been avoided but were sought out instead. An imperialistic nation does not avoid war. It can't be said enough times; an imperialistic nation needs and creates its own enemies for a variety of self-serving interests, and if war ensues, so be it.

7. Conscription?

Would the draft have been abolished after Vietnam if the government was convinced that all future military interventions would be just or necessary? No, the draft was abolished precisely because the government knew future military interventions could not meet those standards and more protests on the magnitude of those against the Vietnam War would surely follow.

8. Exemptions?

The more urgent and just or necessary a war wouldn't there be few exemptions granted from battle? No, in any American war so far the elite have avoided it like a plague. And how many politicians have gone into battle? They are spineless creatures that send others to their graves. They ought to be the pall bearers for every person killed from their wars and then held un-forgivingly accountable.

9. Popularity?

If a particular war were just or necessary, besides not abolishing the draft wouldn't we expect very few conscientious objectors, draft dodgers or deserters? No, just the opposite happened during WWII and Vietnam, the last war relying on conscription. During WWII there were roughly 21,000 deserters (one was executed) and nearly 100,000 conscientious objectors. During Vietnam, there were nearly 4,000 deserters and several hundred thousand draft dodgers. I went to graduate school to keep my school deferment and avoid the risk of going to Vietnam. I'm not a coward, but a pacifist, which actually requires courage in facing war's friends and supporters.

10. Amnesty?

If there was absolutely no question about a particular war being just or necessary, would its warrior-in-chief not have granted conditional or unconditional pardons or amnesty to war resistors over the years? No, in the 20th century over 1,000 draft dodgers during WWII were pardoned by President Truman; Vietnam War draft resisters and deserters were offered clemency by President Ford; and hundreds of thousands of Vietnam War draft dodgers were given unconditional pardon by President Carter. Perhaps even warriors-in-chief can have pangs of doubt or guilt over sending young men to battle.

11. Humanitarian?

What about military interventions for humanitarian reasons, to prevent massacres and to liberate people from ruthless despots, for example? Americans learn in their youth from school textbooks that America always has good intentions towards other nations. [5] But that is sheer propaganda and poppycock deliberately foisted by the power elite on the rest of us to protect their own self interests. No war can be legitimized as well intentioned and humanitarian.

To quote Einstein once again, "War cannot be humanized. War can only be abolished." There should never be inhumane means to a humane end. Rationalizing military interventions as humanitarian interventions "is a sign of progress," David Swanson, author of War is a Lie says, adding, "That we fall for it is a sign of embarrassing weakness. The war propagandist is the world's second oldest profession (David, if you don't mind, I 'm going to call it the fourth oldest profession), and the humanitarian lie is not entirely new. But it works in concert with other common war lies." [6]

Wars do not liberate civilians from oppressors. Wars kill the civilians and tyrants in their lands often follow ruling puppet regimes that suit American regimes' self-interests. Recall in Chapter 1 my mentioning that throughout history wars on the average have killed more civilians than combat soldiers. The civilian casualty rate rose to 85% of all casualties during the Iraq War and probably is approaching 100% from drone killings. [7]

Finding and using a genuinely humane intervention requires creative diplomacy and a moral conscience, not military might.

12. Moral?

I would think that only a psychopath or a diehard war rationalizer would argue that war does not breech one or more of those universal moral values I mentioned in Chapter 2.

13. Legal?

What about the lesser standard for behavior, law? Recall all of those laws I listed in Chapter 2 that are being violated by the U.S. I would think only people like the U.S. president's legal counsel would make the legal case for war, torture, and the like.

And What About Spying?

The answer ought to be self-evident. As an off shoot of the war habit, spying automatically fails the litmus tests.

Conclusion

War can never be just because no war can be morally justified. War can never be necessary because every war neglects or worsens needs of the common people on either side of the war. The only substitute for war is peace.

Endnotes

1. Zinn, H. Howard Zinn on War. Seven Stories Press, 2000.
2. For some evidence that America's regimes create and provoke her enemies see Petras, J. Provocations as Pretexts for Imperial War: From Pearl Harbor to 9/11. Global Research, August 3, 2014; also, Dobbs, M. Ford and GM Scrutinized for Alleged Nazi Collaboration. The

Washington Post, November 30, 1998; and Dietrich, D. The Pearl Harbor Deception. December 2008. http://www.apfn.net/CC29/A001I081207-819a.MP3

3. Zinn, H. Op. Cit. As for the Holocaust, Eli Weise, Nobel Peace Laureate and Holocaust survivor and others have claimed that the Holocaust could have been prevented if appropriate actions would have been taken by the Allies. Weise, for instance, contended that; "It could have been prevented. The greatest tragedy in history could have been prevented had the civilized world spoken up, taken measures in 1939, '40, '41, '42. Each time, in Berlin, Goebbels and the others always wanted to see what would be the reaction in Washington and London and Rome, and there was no reaction so they felt they could continue." Rogin, J. Eli Weise: Why is Assad Still in Powerr? Foreign Policy, April 23, 2012. See also, e.g., LeTraunik, E. The Riegner Telegram. The Jewish Magazine, November 2008; and Groth, AJ. Accomplices: Churchill, Roosevelt and the Holocaust. Peter Lang International Academic Publishers, 2011.

4. Zinn, H. A People's History of the United States. Harper Perennial, 2005, 188.

5. Fitzgerald, F. America Revised: History Schoolbooks in the Twentieth Century. Little Brown & Company, 1979.

6. Rowley, C. Selling War as Smart Power. OpEdNews, August 31, 2012.

7. Eckhardt, W. "Civilian deaths in wartime." Security Dialogue, 2008 (1), 89-98; and Roberts, PC. Why War Is Inevitable. OpENews, May 26, 2014.

APPENDIX B
VOICES AGAINST WAR
DOWN THROUGH THE AGES

Alfred Adler: To all those who walk the path of human cooperation war must appear loathsome and inhuman.

Aeschylus: In war, truth is the first casualty.

Aesop: Any excuse will serve a tyrant.

Anonymous: A great war leaves a country with three armies: an army of cripples, an army of mourners, and an army of thieves.

Issac Asimov: Violence is the first refuge of the incompetent.

Major General Smedley Butler. War is a racket.

Albert Camus: We used to wonder where war lived, what it was that made it so vile. And now we realize that we know where it lives...inside ourselves.

Bennett Cerf: The Atomic Age is here to stay--but are we.

Agatha Christie: One is left with the horrible feeling now that war settles nothing; that to win a war is as disastrous as to lose one.

Clarence Darrow: True patriotism hates injustice in its own land more than anywhere else.

Bob Dylan: Come you masters of war You that build all the guns You that build the death planes You that build the big bombs You that hide behind walls You that hide behind desks I just want you to know I can see through your masks

Barbara Ehrenreich: No matter that patriotism is too often the refuge of scoundrels. Dissent, rebellion, and all-around hell-raising remain the true duty of patriots.

Albert Einstein: The pioneers of a warless world are the youth that refuse military service.

Albert Einstein: Force always attracts men of low morality.

Albert Einstein: The world is a dangerous place, not because of those who do evil, but because of those who look on and do nothing.

Abraham Flexner: Probably, no nation is rich enough to pay for both war and civilization. We must make our choice; we cannot have both.

Benjamin Franklin: There never was a good war or a bad peace.

Chris Hedges: The failure to dissect the cause of war leaves us open for the next installment.

Herodotus: In peace sons bury fathers, but war violates the order of nature, and fathers bury sons.

Martin Luther King, Jr.: Peace is not merely a distant goal that we seek but a means by which we arrive at that goal.

John Lennon: All we are saying is give peace a chance.

Basil O'Connor. The world cannot continue to wage war like physical giants and to seek peace like intellectual pygmies.

Anne O'Hare McCormick: Today the real test of power is not capacity to make war but capacity to prevent it.

Charles Eliot Norton: The voice of protest...is never more needed than when the clamor of fife and drum...is bidding all men...obey in silence the tyrannous word of command.

George Orwell: Freedom is slavery. Ignorance is strength. War is peace.

Harry Patch, Last surviving WWI soldier: War is organized murder, and nothing else.

Alexander Pope: O peace! how many wars were waged in thy name.

Ayn Rand: Do not ever say that the desire to "do good" by force is a good motive. Neither power-lust nor stupidity is good motives.

Jeannette Rankin: You can no more win a war than you can win an earthquake.

Bertrand Russel: War does not determine who is right, only who is left.

Antoine De Saint-Exupery: War is not an adventure. It is a disease. It is like typhus.

Arthur Schopenhauer: All truth passes through three stages. First, it is ridiculed. Second, it is violently opposed. Third, it is accepted as being self-evident.

Butler Shaffer: In this war – as in others – I am less interested in honoring the dead than in preventing the dead.

Bruce Springsteen: Blind faith in your leaders or in anything will get you killed.

Charles V of France: Name me an emperor who was ever struck by a cannonball.

Howard Zinn: We need to decide that we will not go to war, whatever reason is conjured up by the politicians or the media, because war in our time is always indiscriminate, a war against innocents, a war against children.

APPENDIX C
GOVERNMENT'S WAR/SPY
ORGANIZATIONAL CHART

Executive Branch: The War Bureaucracy

Office of the President
  The President
  Chief Counter Terrorism Advisor
  National Security Advisor and Staff
  Office of Digital Strategy
  Office of Legal Counsel
  Office of Legislative Affairs
  Office of National Drug Control Policy
  Office of Science and Technology Policy
  Office of the White House Counsel
  President's Intelligence Advisory Board and Intelligence
Oversight Board
Department of Defense
    Defense Policy Board
    Defense Agencies
        Defense Advanced Research Project
        Defense Intelligence Agency
        Defense Security Service
        Defense Threat Reduction Agency
        Missile Defense Agency
        National Counterterrorism Center
        National Geospatial-Intelligence Agency
        National Reconnaissance Office
        National Security Agency
        Plus Many More
    Field Activity Bureaucracy
        Defense Media Alert
        Plus More
    Joint Chiefs of Staff
        Uniformed Branches

Army + More
Unified Combatant Commands
National Defense University
Special Operations Command
Plus More

Executive Branch: The Spy Bureaucracy

Independent agencies
Central Intelligence Agency
United States Department of Defense
Air Force Intelligence, Surveillance and
Reconnaissance Agency
Army Military Intelligence
Defense Intelligence Agency
Marine Corps Intelligence Activity
Military Intelligence Board
National Security Agency
National Geospatial-Intelligence Agency
National Reconnaissance Office
Office of Intelligence and Analysis
Office of Intelligence and Counterintelligence
Office of Naval Intelligence
United States Department of Energy
Office of Intelligence and Counterintelligence
United States Department of Homeland Security
Office of Intelligence and Analysis
Coast Guard Intelligence
United States Department of Justice
Federal Bureau of Investigation, National Security
Branch
Drug Enforcement Administration, Office of National
Security Intelligence
United States Department of State
Bureau of Intelligence and Research
United States Department of the Treasury

Office of Terrorism and Financial Intelligence

Legislative Branch

Aka: Bureaucracy of Checks and Imbalances Or The Lost and Fund Departments;
"Capital" Hill for the War and Spy Business; and Enriching the War & Spy Business: Impoverishing the Taxpayer

Senate Subcommittee on Defense Appropriations Senate Subcommittee on Homeland Security Subcommittee on Military Construction and Veterans Affairs, and Related Agencies Senate Committee on Armed Services (six subcommittees) Senate Committee on the Budget Senate Committee on Commerce, Science, and Transportation (six relevant subcommittees) Senate Subcommittee on Energy Senate Subcommittee on Clean Air and Nuclear Safety Senate Committee on Finance (two relevant subcommittees) Senate Committee on Foreign Relations (seven subcommittees) Senate Committee on Homeland Security & Governmental Affairs (five subcommittees) Senate Committee on Small Business and Entrepreneurship Senate Committee on Veterans' Affairs The Senate Select Committee on Intelligence Committee

The House Permanent Select Committee on Intelligence (three subcommittees) House Subcommittee on Homeland Security Appropriations House Subcommittee on Defense Appropriations House Subcommittee on Military Construction, Veterans Affairs, and Related Agencies Appropriations House Subcommittee on Financial Services and General Government Appropriations House Subcommittee on State, Foreign Operations, and Related Programs Appropriations House Committee on Armed Services (nine subcommittees) House Committee on

267

Budget House Committee on Energy and   Commerce
(three relevant subcommittees) House Committee on
Foreign Affairs (seven subcommittees) House Committee
on Homeland Security (six subcommittees) House
Committee on Science, Space, and Technology (five
subcommittees) Subcommittee on Technology and
Innovation House Subcommittee on Small Business
Contracting and the Workforce House Committee on
Transportation and Infrastructure (two relevant
subcommittees) House Committee on Veterans' Affairs
(four subcommittees) House Committee on Ways and
Means (oversight committee)

APPENDIX D
THE WAR AND SPY INDUSTRIES

100 Largest Defense Contractors*

Acutronic Accenture Ltd. Action. TargetAdvatech. Pacific, Inc. Aerojet Aerospace Corporation. Aerovironment. Advanced Armament Corporation (AAC). Advanced Integrated Systems. AECOM Aegis Defense Services. Aimpoint. AirScan. Airtronic USA. Aivea Corporation. Allen Vanguard. Alliant Techsystems. Allied Container Systems. AM General Corporation. American Dynamics Flight Systems. American Ordnance LLC. American Petroleum Institute Analysis, Computing & Engineering Solutions, Inc. Antonov Airlines. Applied Research Associates Inc. Arcturus-UAVARINC. Argon ST. Armor Source. Armor Works. Artis LLC. ASSETT, Inc. Astronautics Corporation of America. Aurora Flight Sciences. AV-Optimal Defense Consultancy Service. AVX Aircraft Company. BAE Systems plc. BAE Systems Inc. BAE Systems Land and Armaments. BAE Systems Electronics, Intelligence & Support Land Systems. OMC Ball Corporation. Ball Aerospace & Technologies Corp. Barrett Firearms Manufacturing. Battelle Memorial Institute. Bechtel Corporation. Benelli USABerico Technologies. BDM Corporation. Blazeware Inc. Black Knight Technology Inc. Boeing Company. Boeing Sikorsky Comanche Team. Boeing SVS. McDonnell Douglas. Insitu. Booz Allen Hamilton. Boston Dynamics. British Nuclear Fuels Limited. Brogden Enterprises, Inc. CACI International Inc. Carlyle Group. Carnegie Mellon University. Ceradyne. Charles Stark Draper Laboratory. Chenega Federal Systems. CNA Corporation. Colt. Defense Concurrent Technologies Corporation. Critical Solutions International. Crye Associates. CSA

Engineering. CSI Combined Systems. Computer Sciences Corporation. Cubic Corporation. Omega Training Group. Decibel Research Inc. Defense Technologies Inc. Delta Intelligence & Security. DEW Engineering. Digital System Resources Inc. Dillon Aero. DRS Technologies. DynCorp. Dynetics, Inc. EADS North America. Exnovo Solutions, Inc. Eurocopter. American Eurocopter. Airbus. Earth Class. MailEast/West Industries, Inc. Ensign-Bickford Aerospace and Defense. Edison Welding Elbit Systems Institute. M7 Aerospace. ENSCO, Inc. Environmental Tectonics Corporation. Ernst & Young. Evergreen International Aviation. Exxon Corporation. Fabbrica d'Armi Pietro Beretta. Fabrique Nationale de Herstal. FLIR Systems. Fluor Corp. FGM Inc. FMC Technologies. Force Protection Inc. Foster-Miller, Inc. Foster Wheeler Ltd. Foundation Health Systems Inc. G4S plc. Armour Group Inc. GB Industrial Battery. Gemini Industries Inc. General Atomics. General Dynamics. Gulfstream MOWAG. General Dynamics Electric Boat. Bath Iron Works. General Electric Military Jet Engines Division. Geo-Centers Inc. Glock. Ges.m.b.H. Goodrich Corporation. Gordon and Castille Industries. Georgia Tech Research Institute. Harris Corporation. Halliburton Corporation. Health Net, Inc. Heckler & Koch. USA HESCO. USA Hewlett-Packard. Honeywell. HS Produkt. Humana Inc. Hybricon Corporation. IBM Industrial Machining & Design Services, Inc. Infotech Aerospace Services (a Pratt & Whitney joint venture). Insight Technology. Institute for Defense Analyses. Intelsat International Resources Group. iRobot. Israeli Aerospace Industries. Israeli Military Industries. ITT Exelis. ITT Research Institute Jacobs Engineering Group Inc. JGB Enterprises, Inc. Johns Hopkins University. Kaman Aircraft. Kearfott Corporation. Kellogg, Brown and Root. Knight's Armament Company. Kongsberg Defence & Aerospace. L-3 Communications Holdings, Inc.

SYColeman. Brashear. EOTech. Lockheed Martin. Gyrocam Systems. Longbow Limited Liability Inc. LRAD Corporation. M9 Defense Systems. MacGregor Group (part of Cargotec corporation). A.P. Moller-Maersk Group. ManTech International. Massachusetts Institute of Technology Maytag Aircraft Corporation MBDA. McQ Inc. Menatek Spare Parts. Metal Storm. Milkor USA. Mission Essential. Personne. MITRE Corporation. ANSER Institute for Homeland Security. Mitsubishi. Motorola Inc. Mustang Tech Group. Natel Electronic Manufacturing Services. Navistar Defense. Nextel. NexGen Data Systems, inc. Nichols Research Corporation. Nittoh Kensetsu Co., LTD. Northrop Grumman Corporation. Northrop Grumman Electronic Systems. Northrop Grumman Information Technologies. Northrop Grumman Integrated Systems. Northrop Grumman Mission Systems. Northrop Grumman Newport News. Northrop Grumman Ship Systems. Northrop Grumman Space Technology. Northrop Grumman Technical Services. Ocean Shipholdings Inc. Oceaneering International. Olin Corporation. Orbital Sciences Corporation. Oshkosh Corporation. Osterhout Design Group. OT Training Solutions. Para-Ordnance. Perot Systems. Picatinny Arsenal. Pinnacle Armor. Point Blank Solutions, Inc. Precision Castparts Corporation. Quantum3D. QinetiQ North America. Raytheon. BBN Technologies. JPS Communications. ELCAN Sighting Systems. Remington Arms. Revision Eyewear. Rock Island Arsenal. Rockwell. Collins Rolls-Royce plc. RONCO. Horn of Africa. Saab AB.SBG Technology Solutions. Science Applications International Corporation (SAIC). Sensis Corporation. Shell Oil Company. Siemens. AG. Simplex. Grinnell, LP. SFA, Inc. SGISSmartronix, Inc. SmartRounds. Smith & Wesson. Sobran, inc. SPARTA, Inc. SpotterRF. Springfield Armory. SRC Inc. SRI International. ST Engineering. ST Kinetics. Sumaria

System. Vision Technologies Systems. Stanley, Inc. Standard Missile Company LLC. Stevedoring Services of America. Stewart and Stevenson Strum, Ruger & Company Incorporated. Subsystem Technologies Incorporated. Sverdrup Corporation. Swiss ArmsSIG Sauer Talla-Tech. Tangent Networks LLC. Forjas. Taurus S/A. TCom. Teledyne. Telent. Texas Instruments. Textron Inc. Bell Helicopter. Textron United. Industrial Corporation. AAI Corporation. The Columbia Group. Trijicon. Tri-Star Engineering, Inc. TriWest Healthcare Alliance. Tyco International Ltd. ADT Security Services. University of Texas System. Unisys Corporation. United Technologies. Sikorsky Pratt & Whitney. URS Corporation. Washington Group International. USmax Corporation. US Falcon. US Ordnance. Vangent. Velocity Systems. Verizon Communications. Vinnell Corporation. Vinnell-Brown & Root. Westinghouse Electric Corporation. Wiley X Worldcorp Inc. Wyvern Technologies, Aerospace & Defense Contractors. Academi LLC (formerly Blackwater and Xe Services). York Executive Operations.

----

*This list is from Wikipedia. 2014

Some Major Spy Contractors*

AECOM Tech Corp. Amazon. The Analysis Corporation. BAE Systems/Global Analysis Unit. Battelle Memorial Institute. Boeing Integrated Defense Systems. Booz Allen Hamilton. CACI International, Inc. Capgemini. Carahsoft Technology. Chenega Corp. CSC. General Dynamics. Golder Rauner L.L.C. Griffon Corp. GTCR. Honeywell International. InTTENSITY. Johns Hopkins University. Jorge Scientific Corp. Kingfisher Systems. L-3 Communications. Lockheed Martin - Information Systems and Global Services. ManTech International New World

Solutions. McAfee. Mission Essential. Northrop Grumman. Palantir Technologies Inc. Raytheon Intelligence and Information Systems. SAIC Inc. SI International/Serco. SOS International. Spectal LLC

------

*20014 data. See, e.g., Hollebeek, NJ. Privacy Surveillance. www.hollebeek.nl/rechtslinks. Shorrock, T. Spies for Hire: Who's Who in Intelligence Contractors. Collaborative Research on
Corporations (Crocodyl), November 16, 2009. www.crocodyl.org

About the Author

Gary Brumback received his undergraduate degree from Indiana University and his Ph.D. in organizational psychology from The Ohio State University in 1963. His doctoral dissertation was on the subject of personal and organizational values.

Retired since 1995, Dr. Brumback had a long and varied career involving the retail industry, the insurance industry, the manufacturing industry, university teaching, the not-for-profit research sector, and the U.S. government.

He was elected a Fellow of both The American Psychological Association and The Association for Psychological Science in recognition of his outstanding and distinguished contributions to psychology. He is also a member of Phi Beta Kappa and Sigma Xi.

He is a prolific writer. His first book, Tall Performance from Short Organizations through We/Me Power is about managing performance in non-hierarchical, empowering organizations. He was invited by the U.S. government to showcase his MBR (managing behavior and results) model of performance management around the country. His previous book, The Devil's Marriage: Break Up the Corpocracy or Leave Democracy in the Lurch is about the collusion between big corporations and big government to pursue their own self-interests at the expense of the common good.

He has authored over 50 book reviews, many articles in professional journals, and many technical reports. He has given many talks at professional meetings in the U.S. and abroad. His invited addresses on serious matters have always added a touch of humor. He dressed as "Capt. No

No," for example, in his talk on an oxymoron, "government ethics." His research, writings, and presentations have covered a broad array of topics.

Since retiring he has gone beyond his own field to delve into economics, history, humanism, moral philosophy, political science, public affairs, and theology. He researched all of those subjects to help him write The Devil's Marriage: Break Up the Corpocracy or Leave Democracy in the Lurch, and America's Oldest Professions: Warring and Spying.